John Purcell Fitzgerald

Lay Preaching

A Divinely-Appointed Part of Christian Ministry

John Purcell Fitzgerald

Lay Preaching
A Divinely-Appointed Part of Christian Ministry

ISBN/EAN: 9783337778798

Printed in Europe, USA, Canada, Australia, Japan

Cover: Foto ©Lupo / pixelio.de

More available books at **www.hansebooks.com**

LAY PREACHING:

A Divinely-appointed part of Christian Ministry.

BY

JOHN PURCELL FITZGERALD, M.A.

"Having therefore gifts, differing according to the grace given to us."
ROMANS XII. 6.

"The manifestation of the SPIRIT is given to *every man* to profit withal."
1 CORINTHIANS XII. 7.

LONDON:
WILLIAM HUNT AND COMPANY,
HOLLES STREET, CAVENDISH SQUARE;
AND ALDINE CHAMBERS, PATERNOSTER ROW.
IPSWICH: WILLIAM HUNT, TAVERN STREET.
1873.

PREFACE.

THE writer of these pages would desire to take what he believes is a just middle course between the two extremes that so agitate our devout and earnest Christians. During the last forty years, we have seen the revival of the highest *ministerial* claims—Sacerdotalism, as we must call it—a principle of *entire subjugation by people to the Clergy.* The other extreme may be called *Brethrenism.* That is to say, a Christian republic, in which all believers are equal, not only in regard to spiritual privileges, but almost equal in point of Church official power. A system under which the precept, " *Obey* them that have the rule over you," appears impracticable, for who is to "obey" if none have authority to command, or all may command equally?

It is my object to prove that the ruling Ministers of Churches ought to encourage, and commission, those of their Church who have "gifts" of preaching and teaching, to preach and teach the Gospel to the ignorant around them; and that such ministry was an indispensable part of the Apostolic Church's "order."

CONTENTS.

PART I.

IS LAY PREACHING ALLOWABLE?

PAGE.

The Roman and Greek Churches?—The Church of
England—Article XXV.—Not positively forbidding all
Lay Ministry—The Canons of 1603—The Scotch (Presbyterian) Church: its Elders, but not Evangelists—
Wesley and Whitefield revive the order of Lay Preachers
—Lay Evangelism an integral part of Christian Ministry
—The danger and injury of its past neglect stated—
Delay of the Gospel—Serious Consequences of forbidding Lay Preaching stated—Wesley compelled to make
use of it in 1740—At first opposed to it—Number
of Lay Preachers in the various Methodist bodies—
The religious state of England when Wesley began—
National Immorality—No Gospel in Church Pulpits—
State of Scotland as to Religion—General conclusion—
The religious state of Wales—Howell Harris, the Lay
Evangelist—Ought Wesley, Whitefield, and Harris, to
have forborne thus to Work?—General Conclusion   1—16

CONTENTS.

PART II.

SCRIPTURE PROOFS.

PAGE

General character of this Dispensation (Jer. xxxi.)
—Unordained or Lay Ministry under the later Jewish
Church—As seen in the Apostles' case—No positive
verbal injunctions found in the New Testament for Lay
Preaching—neither for many other important Ordinances
—deemed essential—The first Preachers of the Gospel
at Pentecost : almost all Unordained—Women amongst
them—Objection that no *miracles* can attend or give
authority to Lay Preaching *now*—*Answer* that the
SPIRIT was given for the whole of this Dispensation—
"Greater Works" were to follow the SPIRIT's outpouring upon Pentecost than during our Lord's Mission
—Works of *Conversion* did follow then, and seventeen
centuries later, through the preaching of "Unordained,"
as well as "Ordained" preachers . . 19—25

PART III.

SCRIPTURE TESTIMONY—continued.

The scattered Church, after Stephen's martyrdom,
mostly "unordained" Christians, preach the Word—
Philip, a great preacher, not *ordained* to preach—What
Preaching is—Philip, though unordained, must have
been sanctioned by the Apostles—and was certainly by
the SPIRIT—Philip's Preaching in Samaria—evidently
honoured by the SPIRIT—The preaching of the scattered

CONTENTS. ix

                                      PAGE
(unordained) believers DIVINELY directed—Philip sent by the SPIRIT to the Ethiopian—Recognised afterwards as an Evangelist—*Objection* that Stephen's persecution made Lay Preaching an exceptional work—answered by reference to Ephes. iv.—Evangelist, a gift, separate from that of Pastor, Elder, Deacon, etc.—Bad consequences of neglecting these distinctions . . 29—38

PART IV.

SCRIPTURE TESTIMONY—continued.

THE EPISTLES.

Number and nature of the Epistles—List of "Spiritual Gifts," as stated in the Epistles to Rome and Corinth—Many of the "gifts" not miraculous, but common to the Church in all ages, such as "exhortation"—The Apostles' precept neglected—Prophesying: its double signification—The *practice* of believers at Rome when St. Paul was first imprisoned—Most of the brethren at Rome "preached CHRIST"—Paul did not forbid it, but rejoiced—Notices of believers' teaching and ministry in other Epistles . . . . . 41—50

PART V.

THE MINISTRY OF WOMEN.

May women minister in the Gospels—St. Paul's prohibitions—Qualified by himself in same chapter—They may pray or prophecy *veiled*—The day of Pentecost—

Said to be no precedent—General precepts to all believers to exhort, etc.—To the Colossians and Romans—What it is to "exhort" and "speak" under the Spirit's influence—Special precept to Hebrew Christians—Paul's notice of women labouring in the Gospel—What their labours were—Other women named—Phœbe, a deaconness—Priscilla—Other women—Euodia and Syntyche—Fellow labourers with Clement—The woman of Samaria—Success of her ministry—Greater than that of the Seventy—Mary Magdalene after the Resurrection—The other women—Modern female teachers of the Gospel: Mrs. Stevens, Mrs. Daniells, Mrs. Fry—Conclusion . . . . . 54—67

PART VI.

THE REASONS WHY LAY PREACHING AND TEACHING FELL INTO DISUSE. MINISTERIAL RANK.

True dignity of ministers—in Scripture—False dignities brought in: Bingham's "Christian Antiquities"—The numerous ranks of the Clergy gradually introduced—Ignatius's exaggerated views of Bishops—Wild departure from the Apostle's doctrine—Which standard is to be followed?—Danger of Ignatius's teaching—Clement of Rome, his exaggerated view of obedience to Pastors—Clement's false analogy between the Jewish Priesthood and the Christian Ministry—Clement's views of the "Laity," how different from those of St. Paul—Submission of believers not only to Pastors, but to all who ministered—Why did not St. Paul command absolute submission to himself? . . . 71—83

PART VI.—(2)

CAUSES WHICH LED TO STOP LAY MINISTRY. PRIESTHOOD. REMAINS OF PRIESTHOOD IN THE CHURCH OF ENGLAND.

PAGE.

The Theory of Priesthood traceable in part to Clement of Rome; but he does not call Ministers, *Priests*—He compares Christian Ordinances to Jewish ones—His first letter to Corinthians—He assigns no Ministry to Laymen—Scripture as to the one Sacrifice for Sin—The Eucharist turned into a new Sacrifice—Ignatius —Tertullian—The Roman Catholic view—The *People* under the *Priest*—Error of retaining *Priestly* Titles in the Prayer-book—Cranmer knew the danger—He borrowed from the Romish Ordinal—Error in the Ministerial Commission in Ordination Service—"Visitation of the Sick" Office: its error and danger—Endeavours to defend these Priestly assumptions—Cranmer's and Parker's reasons for retaining these Services—Elizabeth restores objectionable parts of Edward's *first* Prayer-book—Large body of Irish Laymen in the Disestablished Church demanding a "Revision" of Prayer-book—Their Protest . . . . . 87—110

PART VII.

PRESENT MEANS OF GOSPEL INSTRUCTION IN OUR GREAT CITIES INADEQUATE. NEED OF LAY PREACHING.

Ordained Ministers not sufficient to teach our large Populations—Evangelists specially needed—London: its

CONTENTS.

PAGE

Population—Number of the Clergy in London—Number of Nonconformist Ministers—Number of Church and Chapel Sittings—Vast multitudes left practically unevangelized—Is the teaching generally given in Church and Chapel effective?—Improper accommodation given to the poor—Just excuse for masses of the poor not attending—City Missionaries—and Scripture Readers, visitors—Number of Families probably visited—Open-air Preachers—Theatre Preachings—Manchester: its Population—Number of Clergy and Nonconformist Ministers—Number of Sittings in Church or Chapel—City Missionaries, Readers, etc.—Number of People left untaught—Advantage of City Missionaries—Still the Spiritual Destitution remains—to be met by a fresh and well-ordered *Evangelism* . . . 113—131

PART VIII.

APPEAL TO THE GENTRY.

Reflections suggested by the sight of our people—Extract from the *Times* Newspaper of Oct. 12th, 1871, as to necessity and Scriptural duty of Lay Preaching—Final appeal to the *Gentry*—Great importance of their coming forward . . . . . 135—147

PART I.

Lay Preaching: Is it Allowable?

LAY PREACHING.

PART I.

Lay Preaching : Is it Allowable?

MAY unordained men preach the Gospel to the ignorant and neglected, or may they publicly exhort and arouse nominal professors of religion?

These are serious questions. By a large number of Episcopal clergymen such preaching is deemed unauthorized and sinful. It is a thrusting of oneself into "the priest's office." It is even to become a follower of "Korah, Dathan, and Abiram." Those who thus act, shall "perish in the gainsaying of Corah." (Jude.) According to this theory not only unordained laymen, but men who have been ordained by a "Presbytery" and the ministers. Thus the ministers of almost all "Reformation" Churches are equally unwarranted intruders. Their Presbyterian "orders" are not valid. On the other hand, these same Episcopal clergy are equally deemed "unlawful intruders" by the Roman Catholic Church: their "orders" are null and void; and by parity of reasoning, the English clergyman is amongst KORAH's company.

I know that by many eminent Roman Catholic writers, the validity of the Anglican "orders" is admitted: nevertheless, every Englishman who secedes to the Romish priesthood is obliged to be "ordained" afresh; so that his previous ordination goes for nothing.

Such is the view taken by the Roman and Greek Churches. All preaching or evangelism is by them limited to ordained priests, except when, on certain occasions, an order of "preaching friars" has been sent out upon some special mission. These friars and monks were not necessarily ordained by bishops. Thus, in former days, they preached "crusades" against Mahometans in Palestine, or "crusades" against the Waldensian "heretics" in Europe, who threw off the Papacy. So now we believe that monks and friars, as lay-brothers, are sent out on *missions* to Roman Catholics, in order to stir up their faith in the truths of their religion.

As to Church of England teaching on this subject (lay preaching), the twenty-third Article forbids "any one to take upon him the office of public preaching, or of administering the Sacraments in the congre-

IS IT ALLOWABLE? 5

gation, before he be lawfully called and sent forth," etc., etc. By the "congregation," the people assembling in the parish church are the "congregation" intended. When these "Articles" were first drawn up, no religious meetings but those of the Established Church were permitted. Any one who studies the "canons" that were put forth under James I. (in 1604 A.D.), will see the full vigour of the exclusive Church system then set up.

By the Canons of 1603, all meetings for prayer and teaching that are dissentient from the Established Church, are classed and condemned with those of "Popish recusants." (See the fourteen first Canons.) It is a disgrace to our National Church that such odious laws as these should be still retained even *in name*. In *practice* we know that they are repealed, and even become illegal; but they stand, like the old rusted instruments of torture in the Tower of London, to show how far a *Protestant* Church could tread in the persecuting steps of that Rome from which it had separated. Nowhere, indeed, does the twenty-third Article distinctly forbid all preaching on all occasions by laymen. No provision is however made for such preaching, and certainly all custom and tradition have been against it for 300 years. The clergyman has been viewed as the depositary of all the "gifts" of teaching, preaching, and pastorship. All has been "headship" and autocracy. The people, or body, have been stunted and decrepid through inaction.

In the "Church of Scotland," and in many foreign Protestant Churches, "elders" are appointed to a subordinate ministry; and so in our "Congregational" Churches, "deacons" are set apart for much the same purpose: but in all these cases, these "elders" and "deacons" only do their work *within* the Church to which they belong. We hear of no order of "evangelists," or preachers, as sent out by any of these Churches into the desert places of sin around them, until from A.D. 1739 and onwards.

Wesley and Whitefield were then (by the DIVINE mercy) raised up in England; Howell Harris, the noble lay evangelist, was raised up in Wales; then the brothers Haldane (fifty years later) were raised up in Scotland. Of the mighty effects that followed the ministry of these apostolic men, I shall have much to say afterwards. All who have read England's religious history during the last 150 years, know that Wesley's mission was as much carried out by *unordained* preachers as by regularly appointed ministers. Howell Harris was unordained throughout his life. The brothers Haldane, during their first and most successful itinerating journeys of preaching through Scotland, were unordained, though afterwards one of them was set apart as pastor of a church. (See their ably-written and deeply-interest-ing "Lives," by Alexander Haldane, Esq., *seventh edition.*)

But we turn to HOLY SCRIPTURE, in the New Testament,—to the teaching and practice of Apostles, as guided by "the HOLY GHOST sent down from heaven." Does HOLY SCRIPTURE forbid or command the preaching and teaching of DIVINE truth by men not set apart, by imposition of hands, to continued ministry and pastorship ?

We maintain that, from the whole tenour of the New Testament, *all men whose hearts have been filled with a* SAVIOUR's *love, and whose lives correspond to their faith, are called, according to their ability and opportunity, to speak of that* SAVIOUR *to the ignorant and neglected around them.* We maintain that believers may lawfully thus preach and teach without giving up their worldly callings, or being *set apart* for the ministry alone. We maintain that this "lay preaching" or teaching became, in the Apostolic Churches, an integral part of ministry : that the constant forbidding and hindering of lay preaching, in after ages, has been a constant "quenching of the SPIRIT : " that it has incalculably *delayed* the Gospel's progress amidst our fellow men. We say "incalculably delayed;" for it is said of Infinite Wisdom HIMSELF, that "HE could do not many mighty works there, because of their unbelief." (Matt. xiii. 58.) HIS SPIRIT has also declared that man's unbelief and man's unfaithfulness do hinder and delay the promised mercy. (See Isaiah xlviii. 18.) "O that thou hadst hearkened to MY commandments! then had thy peace been as a river, and thy righteousness as the waves of the sea: thy seed also had been as the sand, and the offspring of thy bowels as the gravel thereof; his name should not have been cut off nor destroyed from before Me." By this cold system we maintain that thousands of loving hearts have been checked in their efforts to bless mankind. And, lastly, that we cannot, and ought not, to expect great religious movements by the SPIRIT of GOD upon our peoples, while we neglect to make use of the means set before us: even *the setting to work by people as well as by ministers for the salvation of souls,*—people or laymen, as well as ministers,—to work for the saving of souls, through the use of any gift of teaching or preaching which laymen may possess.

Before closing these remarks, I would state the issue to which we are brought by those who object to all lay preaching, or who deem it irregular and dangerous. We do not deny the faults into which many lay preachers fall. These are easily observed. We speak of the abstract right and duty of laymen to preach and teach. The theory of those who deny that obligation amounts to *this*: However wide-spread be irreligion and wickedness around you, it is not for an unordained gentleman, tradesman, or labourer, to lift up a public warning to those "perishing for lack of knowledge." It is rather the DIVINE will (for to this awful conclusion we must come) that men should perish in sin, unwarned and unevangelized, rather than that unordained men should "help to save them!" Before a man adopts that terrible conclusion, he may well, upon his knee before GOD, look into that eternity to which his own soul, as well as the souls of his fellow-creatures, are drawing so near. He will then, I believe, stay His hand from forbidding "lay preaching."

Before adopting so terrible an alternative, let us also calmly judge of the great religious movement brought about in this country by certain known causes. We may say, with all soberness, that the great "Revival" of spiritual religion throughout England, Wales, and Scotland, which followed Wesley's, Whitefield's, and their companions' preaching, *would never have occurred without their evangelism.* Would the Established clergy, or the Nonconformists of that day, have ever roused England with a living Gospel? And if they could not do it, who could but the great Methodist preachers? And lay preaching was an essential instrument in this holy war.

If lay preaching be such open disobedience of Divine law, how comes it that such untold spiritual good has crowned, and is crowning the disobedient? The Gospel pervades all England. To what other cause (mediately) can we ascribe it, except to the true one: viz., this "Second Reformation" (as we may call it) in England, brought about by those martyr spirits who braved all persecution in order to hold fast the *life of spiritual religion in the soul*,—the only religion worthy of its name?

The vindication of "lay preaching" as a *necessary* part of Christian ministry has been long since unanswerably made. In 1742 Wesley set it forth in his own clear and common-sense way. Fifty years later it was also most convincingly defended by the brothers Haldane when they set out in 1793 on their preaching journeys through Scotland. Wesley himself was at first *opposed* to lay preaching; such was the force of his early habits and education. But necessity, humanity, and love, broke through "the traditions of men." We have his description of his early views upon the subject given by his able biographer, the Rev. L. Pyerman. Through Wesley's teaching, a young servant, named Thomas Markfield, was brought to believe with adoring love "the truth as it is in JESUS." He appears to have travelled for a time as a servant with Charles Wesley. Being left for a time in London, and having begun to preach with great power and blessing, we read that "John Wesley hurried back to London for the purpose of stopping him." Wesley's venerable mother, however, met her son upon his arrival with these memorable words: "John, take care what you do with respect to that young man. He is *as surely called of* GOD *to preach as you are!*" Thenceforwards Markfield, the servant, became one of the most successful evangelists; but he was never "*ordained*" by the "laying on of hands." And how from the first lay preaching of John Cormick and Markfield has the spring swelled into a mighty river of spiritual good to countless souls! In England alone we learn that there are 11,804 lay preachers in the present year ministering throughout the great Methodist body. In foreign lands, and at missionary stations, the number of lay workers, including lay preachers, is 20,000. Amongst the Primitive Methodists at home and abroad were reckoned, in 1868, about 14,000 lay preachers. (See Preface to "Wesley's Life and Times." Vol. i., pp. 3—6.)

Reflect, then, what was the religious state of our country 130 years ago? England, Wales, and Scotland were, for the most part, sunk in vice, ignorance, and nominal religion. We need not dwell long upon a fact so often proved and described. Fielding's disgusting novels were approved by masses of our gentry. Drunkenness and gross swearing were as common amongst them as they are now avoided and condemned. Duels were fought upon many trifling provocations. Sunday Schools had not then been thought of for the children of our poorer brethren. Greenwich and Bartholomew fairs were more like heathen orgies than the rational amusement of a Christian people; while cock-fighting, bear-baiting, and other cruel sports, delighted the rich as well as the poor. Hogarth's celebrated series of pictures fitly illustrated the vice amongst our higher, and the brutality amongst our poorer classes.

From English and Scotch pulpits a cold morality was preached; but it was not the blessed source of holy love to GOD by souls freely forgiven and reconciled. The GOSPEL had departed from our country. Nominal Protestantism, and nominal Churchmanship, had wrapt our people in their deadly sleep. By the few clergymen and Nonconformists who were earnest in their religion, historical "evidences" for the truth of our LORD's DIVINE advent on earth, and defences of HIS DIVINITY, were frequent subjects of pulpit teaching. This was to counteract the wide-spread unbelief in the great verities of Revelation which had set in, and which, like thick black clouds, had so hidden the sun's light from our land.

Brought up in childhood amongst those who called all "Methodists" fanatics, and a spiritual renewal of the soul, or "conversion to God," as madness, I can well recollect the current epithet which well-meaning people attached to a man whose heart and life became awakened to devoted piety: "He is *bitten*" (as by the venom of a mad animal). "I trust no child of mine *will ever be so bitten.*" As for Scotland, we may judge of the state of the Established Church by one fact. It was a matter of debate in the General Assembly (in 1796) "*whether it was a duty to send the Gospel to the heathen.*" As to the Scotch clergy in general, "many of them were genuine Socinians; many of them were ignorant of theology as a system, and utterly careless about the merit of any creed or confession.... To deliver a Gospel sermon, or preach to the heart and conscience of a dying sinner, was as completely beyond their power as to speak in the language of angels." (See "*Lives* of the Haldanes," pp. 122, 123.) From the same work we learn that, in some cases, communicants who had been shut out from Church-membership on account of some gross immorality, *paid money as commutation of their* "PEN-ANCE," *or exclusion*, and were thus reinstated! So had the once stern anti-Popish Church of Knox relapsed into the extreme of Popish "indulgences."

What was the state of Wales and the Welsh Established Church when Howell Harris, an unordained man, braved all persecution in order to evangelize it? The writer of "Wesley's Life and Times" thus draws the picture of Wales at that time: "The morals of the Welsh were deplorably corrupt. In this respect there was no difference between rich and poor, ministers and people. Gluttony, drunkenness, and licentiousness were prevalent. In the pulpits of parish churches the name of CHRIST was scarcely ever uttered," etc. (Vol. i., p. 220, of "Life and Times of Wesley.") The established clergy, had they been enlightened teachers of the Gospel, were ignorant of the language in which most of the Welsh people then spoke. In the pulpit, therefore, those ministers were unto their flocks (as St. Paul says) "barbarians." Such a state of things was in part the result of the "Act of Uniformity." By that Act all religious freedom and zeal had been fettered down, like the stump of Nebuchadnezzar's tree, "with a band of brass and iron." Let any one who contrasts the Wales of to-day—its chapels everywhere teeming with congregations, and the religious life of that people,—let any one contrast these with the Wales of 1739: will he deny that the ministry of an *unordained* man, HOWELL HARRIS, called down most signally the DIVINE sanction and blessing?

All this may be sullenly admitted as a fact, as cause and effect; and yet shall we be told that Wesley, Whitefield, and Harris, *ought* to have prayed, waited, and *believed* that *sufficient zealous clergymen would be soon raised up to do all* the good work? The answer is obvious: "We are not to put off or neglect the doing of known duties because other men neglect to do theirs. We are not to wait idly because others are idle. Besides this, we deny the proposition that the established clergy are the only DIVINELY-appointed preachers of the Gospel in our kingdom. And we moreover say that the most practical way of stirring up the established clergy to the doing of their duty, was for Wesley and Whitefield, Harris and the Haldanes, to prosecute their great mission. This, their theory, was fully justified by what followed." If we would stir up others to do good, let us begin by doing it vigorously ourselves. Through the efforts of these great men, hundreds of the established clergy were aroused to live and teach the pure Gospel faith throughout England, Wales, and Scotland; and to bring on such a "revival" of Gospel truth in Church pulpits, as had never been in our country since the days of Charles II. *Then* three thousand godly ministers were found who gave up their "livings," rather than shipwreck their consciences by subscribing the "Act of Uniformity."

But we cannot stop here. The living stream that gushed forth in the middle of last century, went on widening and deepening itself, till it broke out into all the grand missionary rivers which now flow to various heathen lands. Five great English Missionary Societies alone received, during the years 1867—1868, the sum of *more than half a million* for sending CHRIST's Gospel to the heathen; while nine smaller societies raised the total to £605,101. Scotland spent, during the same year, £58,017 for heathen missions; thus raising the total to £663,118 *for the preached Word.* (See the "Christian Year Book," 1868.) On the other hand, during the year 1870-71, the British and Foreign Bible Society received more than £217,000 for the purposes of printing in all languages, and circulating through all nations, the SCRIPTURES of GOD. During its sixty-seventh year, that Society has issued 3,900,000 copies (in whole or in part) of the inspired Word; and since its formation in 1803, the Society has printed 63,299,738 copies. "This time it shall be said, 'What hath GOD wrought?'"

PART II.

Scripture Testimony as to Lay Preaching.

PART II.

Scripture Testimony as to Lay Preaching.

(1) *The general character of this Christian dispensation, as well as of that which preceded it,* is the mutual teaching of our neighbour in the truth of GOD by all who know that truth. Jeremiah foretells of the coming restoration of Israel to the favour of GOD and to their own land: "They shall no more teach every man his neighbour, and every man his brother, saying, Know ye the Lord." (Jer. xxxi.) These words assume that before that glorious day men *ought* to teach their neighbour, if their neighbour is ignorant; and that if we do not teach our ignorant neighbour, we are plainly disobeying a DIVINE command.

(2) Under the later Jewish period, and during the time of our DIVINE LORD's first advent, no "ordination" by laying on of hands was given to the public teachers of the Law of God, such as the scribes and doctors of whom we so often read in

the New Testament: "The scribes and the Pharisees sit in Moses' seat." (Matt. xvi. 1.) In a special way, and by virtue of their office, the consecrated "priests" were to be teachers of the people: "The priests' lips should keep knowledge, and they should seek knowledge at his mouth; for he is the messenger (angel) of the LORD of hosts." (Mal. ii. 9, and Deut. xxxiii.)

But teaching was not limited to priests. "The scribes and the Pharisees sit in Moses' seat:" and rigid as was that Mosaic code, it is certain that in all the synagogue meetings, or meetings of professed worshippers of GOD, any Jew might exhort his brethren out of the Law and Prophets, he being without *outward* commission to do so through the imposition of hands by elders or rulers of synagogues. Throughout His blessed life, the LORD of glory was never arraigned on a charge of violating Church order, because He taught in their synagogues without outward induction by men's hands to such ministry. I find this fact adduced by John Wesley, as a vindication of lay preaching under the Gospel. Thus, then, liberty of teaching (or preaching) was given under the law to every devout man. "Brethren, if any of you have any word of exhortation, say on," was the invitation given to Paul and Barnabas in the synagogue of Antioch. (Acts xiii.) Have unordained ministers, then, under the glorious Gospel, less liberty to exhort and expound Scripture (*i.e.*, *preach*) than Jews under the law? I see no doubt but that the Apostles' Church-meetings, and the rulers and "elders" who governed them, were modelled 'on the Jewish synagogue. Liberty to utter prayer before the congregation, and to "prophecy,"—that is, to "speak unto exhortation and edification and comfort,"—was allowed to all in due subordination. (1 Cor. xiv.) But we shall see this point more and more fully proved when we come to the Apostles' time.

To the New Testament, to the words of our LORD and of HIS apostles, and to the practice of those apostles, we must go for fullest information and for decision. Positive commands, in so many words, to unordained brethren to preach, are certainly *not to be found in Scripture*. Neither have we plain commands that single elders or bishops should continue to preside over large districts or dioceses, that infants should be baptized, or that the people of a Church should elect and dismiss their ministers, etc. No positive verbal command exists for changing the Jewish Sabbath to the first day of the week. And so in very many other cases. Take only one more: it is perhaps to us the most remarkable. Binding as we feel the duty of giving the Bible to all men, we can find no positive command in that DIVINE book for so doing. We feel however this duty to be paramount. We are "to do good to all men;" and this is truly to do them good.

The first great preachers of the Word were mostly unordained men and women. On the day of Pentecost we read that the 120 believers, "with the women" (named in chapter i. of the "Acts"), were "filled with the HOLY GHOST;" and that they spoke in other tongues, "as the SPIRIT gave them utterance," the "wonderful works of GOD." (Acts ii. 11.) What "works" could these be? Not the mechanism of the stars, nor of "the laws of nature;" but of the wonderful work of GOD: a DIVINE SAVIOUR becoming man; obeying, dying, rising, for man; ascending to send the SPIRIT down upon men; and thus to prove incontestably to man that HE fulfilled from heaven the promise which HE had made on earth.

All these "servants and handmaidens" on whom the SPIRIT fell, thus became so far preachers of "the Word." Through their preaching, as much or far more than by Peter's explanation of the Scriptures, was the multitude who came together, arrested, alarmed, and "goaded to the heart." Women as well as men here spoke or preached, "as the SPIRIT gave them utterance." How many they were in number, we are not told. A few only of the holy women are named in Luke viii., as followers of CHRIST; and a few only are named in Acts i.: "With the women, and Mary the mother of JESUS." Such is their description. It will be however said, "Pentecost was a time of miracle: all was then extraordinary. No precedent can thence be drawn, as it regards our present state, nor any fair argument for the preaching of the Gospel by unordained men. Those who spoke on Pentecost were inspired by God. Their utterance was an irresistible outflow of Divine truth. *We* have to do with *uninspired* teachers. *We* depend on human learning,—great knowledge of Scripture,—in order to make a man fit to preach."

We answer, We know that we have no miracles to help our unordained preachers, yet, if it should please God in His mercy to enable many unordained men to preach His Word in days past, or on one day, "in demonstration of the Spirit and of power," to the enlightening and conversion of thousands,—if God be pleased to fill "unlettered" as well as "unordained" men, with heavenly zeal and power to persuade and awaken the ungodly, how can we say that the gifts of Pentecost are all withdrawn, or that no extraordinary powers of preaching and teaching shall return, or have returned? I believe that the Pentecostal outpouring was intended to last throughout this whole dispensation. "They shall prophecy *in those days.*" I have myself heard during the last year, rough Scotch fishermen, who toil the six weekly days upon the sea, preach with a power that I scarcely ever felt in the ministry of any college-educated or ordained minister. I could only wish that our Manchester brethren of the factories and coal-pits could hear those "sons of thunder" speak. And was not extraordinary power, as great as that of Pentecost, given, when George Whitefield preached to 18,000 and 20,000 souls at one time; or when John Cennick, Thomas Marsfield, and Howell Harris, all *unordained* men, preached to thousands, and turned thousands from the "wrath to come," to find their heaven in CHRIST? Were not these "miracles of grace" in the last century?

If, then, we be told that Pentecost is no precedent, for it was a time of miracle, I confess that "speaking with foreign tongues" (as on that day), is to my mind a less miracle than the *conversion of ungodly men through these fishermen's preaching*. It is against human calculation, and against the traditional teaching which learned ministers give us. The greatest of miracles is wrought through such preaching. It is a miracle without and above mere "signs and wonders:" *the salvation of souls by means of rough uneducated teachers.*

Upon Pentecost, 3,000 souls were raised to an heavenly life; and 1,700 years afterwards, by the same SPIRIT, and through the preaching of the same Gospel, thousands on thousands more rose from their death of sin and formalism in England, Scotland, and North America. And "greater" were these latter "works" of conversion than those of

Pentecost. Wesley, Whitefield, and Harris, could work no outward "signs and wonders," such as often followed or went before the Pentecostal preachings. It was GOD's mighty power, more gloriously set forth to save souls by the Word of HIS Gospel, without *works* of miracle. Not a blind man received eye-sight, nor a lame man strength; but the "foolishness of *preaching*," and that often by men "unlearned," "was the instrument of saving them that believed." Upon one day George Whitefield, after one out-door preaching, received a thousand letters from persons who were anxiously inquiring, "What must I do to be saved?"

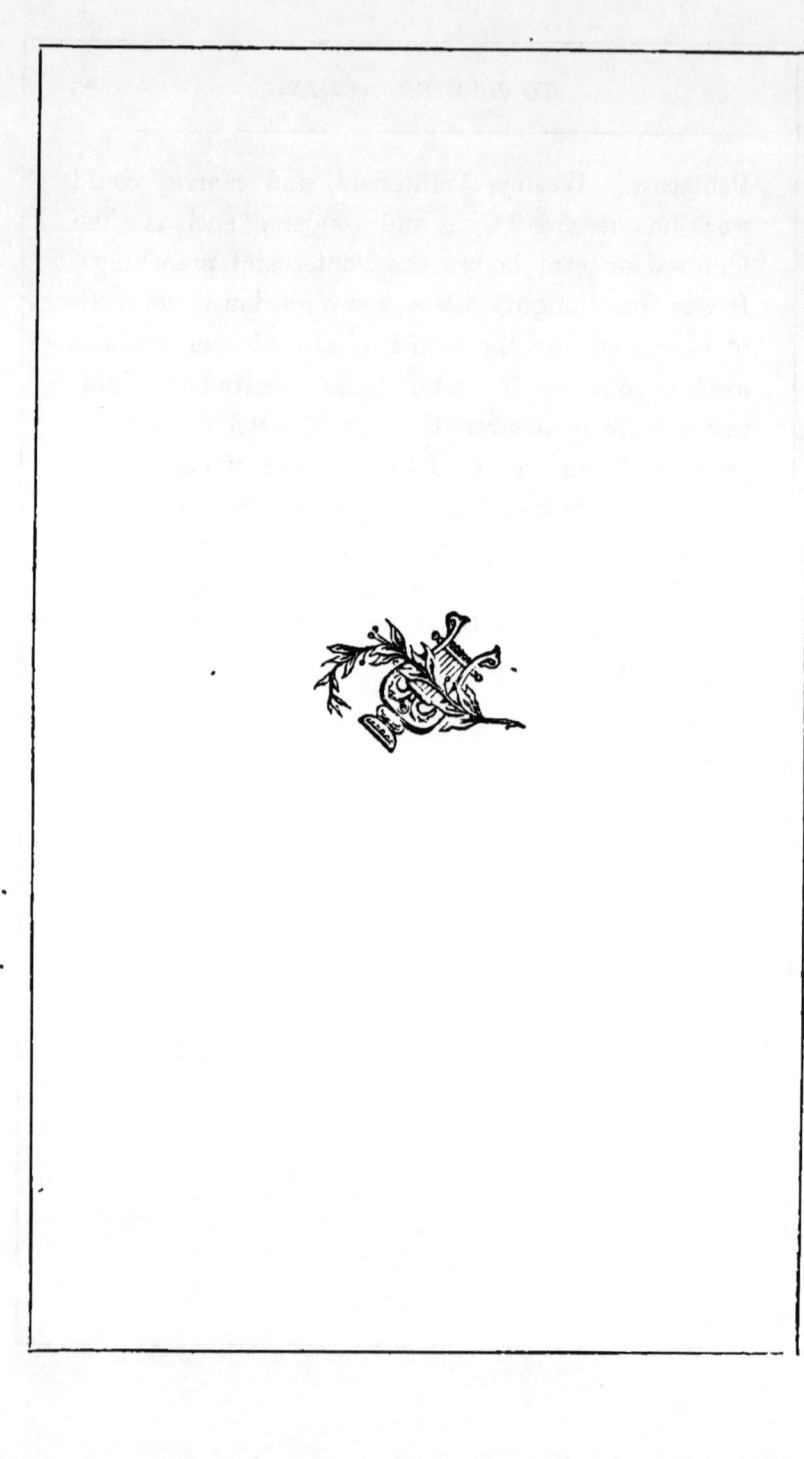

PART III.

*Scripture Testimony as to Lay Preaching
—continued.*

PART III.

Scripture Testimony as to Lay Preaching —continued.

The second great success of the preaching of believers un-ordained, and not set apart for that exclusive work of ministry, was after the martyrdom of Stephen. In Acts viii. 1, we read, that "there was a great persecution of the Church that was at Jerusalem; and they were all (the Church) scattered abroad throughout the regions of Judæa and Samaria, except the Apostles." (Ver. 1.) And in ver. 4, "They that were scattered abroad went every where *preaching the Word.*" This scattered "multitude" must have embraced many thousand men and women. From Acts v. 4, we learn that in Jerusalem alone the believers amounted to five thousand: *i.e.*, that *all* these went forth preaching the Word, the text declares. By this we suppose that, according to his or her ability and "spiritual gift," each believer spoke to or exhorted those whom they met upon their journey. "Preaching" does not consist in a man's addressing a crowd, no more than in a loud, long, or elaborate appeal. Paul "preached" when he conversed with a few women at the river side, when he explained Scripture within the synagogue of Antioch, or when he poured forth his appeal to the crowd upon Mars' Hill. (Acts xvii.) So, again, Philip "preached" JESUS to his one hearer the Eunuch. (Acts viii. 35.) We have no right to suppose that before they left Jerusalem, these two or three thousand believers were set apart by imposition of hands, or what we call "ordination." Most certain it is that the *women*, who must have formed a large part of the company, were not so ordained, and perhaps half of the number were women. There is no evidence for it. In regard to one of their number, Philip by name, greater success attended his "preaching of Christ" to the Samaritans than seems to have followed that of the Apostles at any given place or time, except on Pentecost. (Acts viii. 5—8.) "The people with one accord gave heed unto the things that Philip spake, hearing and seeing the miracles which he did." But we know (from Acts vi.) that Philip had not been "ordained" to preach the Gospel. With six other brethren was he appointed to minister to poor widows. Whereas "we will give ourselves to prayer and to the ministry of the Word," said the Apostles. This limited office, however, of almsgiving for bodily wants, was not to check the outflowing of Philip's loving heart towards men's souls. Philip, when he had done his daily work (if it was daily), went forth "preaching the Word." "Samaria" was to receive the message of life next to Judæa. In Acts i., the Apostles were told, "Ye shall be witnesses unto Me both in Jerusalem, and in all Judæa, and in Samaria, and unto the uttermost part of the earth." Yet those eleven Apostles were not personally nor literally to be the first witnesses in Samaria: Philip was to do that work. Is it not plain that by so acting Philip believed himself to be a partaker in the Apostles' great commission, "Preach the good tidings to every creature"? According to our traditional views, Philip took a great responsibility upon himself, presuming to go before the Apostles,—"running," as we should say, "before he was sent." How can we explain such daring "*irregularity*," such breach of "Church order" (as we hear it often called), for the unordained to strike boldly into an unevangelized mass? We answer: PHILIP's *preaching must have been sanctioned, approved, and commended, if not expressly commanded.* This we prove unanswerably (1) by the marvels of DIVINE power and blessing which followed his preaching; unaccountable, all of them, if he was *sinning.* (2) Never do we find PHILIP blamed or discouraged by the Apostles. They had no jealous fear that his "preaching" would be more successful than their own: nor do we find any of the two or three thousand brethren who tried to "preach the Word" reproved or silenced, as we doubtless should now discourage young and inexperienced brethren. According to the after notions of "Church order," all such preaching would be deemed "raw" and dangerous. "Preaching is a holy science," it is said: "only to be ventured on after long years of study and of prayer."

To whose practice then shall we look as a pattern? Shall it be to that of Apostles, who were DIVINELY guided in all their great movements; and who, thus guided, approved this preaching by the scattered brethren? Or shall we take as our pattern the practice of the Churches, as we have seen it to be in subsequent ages?

(2) I have here taken the case of Philip as being sufficient in itself to justify the 2,000 or 3,000 unordained evangelists. But the Word of God does thus fully describe it (turn to Acts xi. 19—21): "They which were scattered abroad upon the persecution that arose about Stephen, travelled as far as Phenice, and Cyprus, and Antioch, preaching the Word to none but unto the Jews only. *And the hand of the* LORD *was with them: and a great number believed, and turned unto the* LORD." Here then, if ever, was there a clear DIVINE sanction and approval of unordained man's efforts

to honour the SAVIOUR and to save souls: "The hand of the LORD," HIS life-giving SPIRIT, was "with them,"—these scattered, travelling preachers. These unordained men, mostly poor men, ignorant and unlearned in worldly "letters" or "education," as the Fishermen Peter and John manifestly were. (Acts iv. 6.)

Whether many others of the scattered brethren worked miracles, as did Philip, and thus helped forward their own preaching "by signs following," we are not told. Whether they wrought miracles or not, our position remains unchanged: viz., the DIVINE approval of *unordained* preachers of the Gospel. And if such unordained preaching was sanctioned, and we must say *appointed*, then why is it not sanctioned and appointed for our times, for all times,—for all times in which men are "enemies to GOD by wicked works," and need to be taught the way of life?

Moreover, to remove all doubt as to the DIVINE approval of Philip and the others unordained to evangelistic work, we must go on to the sequel of his history, in Acts viii. 26. An angel of GOD is sent to commission him to "preach Christ" to an Ethiopian officer, aud through that officer to send the "glad tidings" to the north of Africa. "The SPIRIT said unto Philip, Go, join thyself to his chariot." (Verse 29.) "Philip opened his mouth, ... and began at the same Scripture, and preached unto him JESUS."

(Verse 35.) Moreover, if we pass on to Acts xxi. 8, we shall find this holy, zealous preacher termed by the HOLY SPIRIT "Philip the Evangelist,"—the title plainly of a recognized office-bearer in the Church.

Still it will be urged, "At that first beginning of the Christian Church, regular Church order was not yet set up. Fifty years later full Church order came in. Besides, if this 'persecution' after Stephen's death had not arisen, these unordained brethren would never have gone from their homes, nor left their family duties, to go out preaching. You must turn to the Epistles of Paul to Timothy and Titus: you will there see that only two orders of ministers were to be set apart for teaching DIVINE truth to men: the 'elder,' or 'bishop' (1 Tim. iii. 1—7; Titus i. 5—9); and the 'deacon,' or subordinate 'minister.' (1 Tim. iii. 8.) Church order existed when bishops, pastors, and deacons, got into their settled offices within the Churches. We read then of no such irregular preachings; nor do we read of unordained men travelling to a distance to preach."

Our answer to these objections is—

What you call a "settled state of the Churches," is best tested, as we judge, by the DIVINE Epistles. In Eph. iv., then, we read, that "HE gave some, apostles; and some, prophets; and some, *evangelists;* and some, pastors and teachers; for the perfecting of the saints, for the work of the ministry, for the edifying of the body of CHRIST: till we all come in the unity of the faith, unto a perfect man."

The figures now used by the SPIRIT: viz., a growing building and a body, show what ministries were to end, and what were to continue throughout our present "dispensation."

"Apostles" and "Prophets" are the beginning of the building: "Ye are built on the *foundation* of the apostles and prophets." That foundation has been *once for all* laid. "Evangelists, pastors, and teachers," on the contrary, must continue their ministry, in order to gather in souls.

The office of "Evangelist" is here plainly distinguished from that of "pastor" and "teacher." Just so are all these three offices distinguished from that of an *Apostle*. It is generally admitted that "apostles" and "prophets," in the full and strict sense of those offices, were no longer given, nor intended to be given to the Churches, after what we call the "Apostolic age." Of course we know that the POPE of ROME is deemed by Roman Catholics as complete successor of PETER, though he aspires to powers infinitely above those which Peter had received. By what are called "Anglo-Catholics and Greek-Catholics,"—bishops who can trace a lineal descent to the original Apostolic ordination,—are in an especial degree "successors of the Apostles;" and by the laying on of such bishops' hands, the

Holy Ghost is still given. (Acts viii. 18.) We believe that such a power was given to the Apostles alone. They had "seen the Lord" visibly after His resurrection. (1 Cor. ix. 1.) They alone were guided "into all the truth" (John xiv. 26), in order to become inspired teachers of men.

In these three great characteristics, Apostles have no successors. In vain then do men call themselves "Apostles' successors," if they have not these three above-named credentials to show, nor any of them. But "evangelists," or "messengers of good tidings," are a perpetual ordinance in the Church of Christ, just as well as are "pastors and teachers." That is to say, as long as masses of ignorant men need the "glad tidings" to be brought to them, so long must "evangelists" be needed to carry those glad tidings to them. The world's wide misery, sin and ignorance, prove the need of evangelism: that is to say, preaching of the Gospel as distinct from the work of "pastors and teachers" within their own Churches. Evangelists may be called the Church's *outdoor* workers for the salvation of the outside world,—the constant goers into the "highways and hedges." Such evangelists are, I believe, especially the "angels," or "messengers," who were to be "sent forth with the sound" of the Gospel trumpet, "to gather in" sheaves of the elect "from the four winds of heaven." (Matt. xxiv. 31.)

Let us not be mistaken. Though the offices of

pastor and evangelist be distinct, the gifts peculiar to both offices may be combined in the same person. St. Paul combined them when he stayed for two whole years with the Church of Ephesus. (Acts xix. 10.) "These taught you publicly, and from house to house" (Acts xx. 20); and appointing elders, "overseers" (bishops), and "deacons" were continually to "preach the Word," and to "do the work of an *evangelist*." Still it is plain that in most cases "pastor" and "evangelist" were not combined, no more than were the "deacon" and "pastor." Yet how lost have been these distinctions amongst ourselves, and indeed ever since the Churches fell from Apostolic rule! And yet how common is the remark, "Such a minister is an excellent pastor, a kind visitor, and private teacher of his people; but he is *no preacher*." Or, again: "He is great in the pulpit, but he is not fitted for mere pastoral work," etc. We wonder not at this unequal (as we call it) distribution of gifts: they were not meant to belong to the same man. "To *one* is given by the SPIRIT the word of knowledge; to *another* (not to the same) the word of wisdom by the same SPIRIT." (1 Cor. xii. 8.) And in Romans xii. 6—8, how clear! "Having then gifts DIFFERING *according to the grace that is given to us*, whether prophecy, let us prophecy; or he that exhorteth, on exhortation," etc. If the Churches planted by Apostles were meant to be in any sense our examples, what "order" of ministry do we find in them? Certainly *not* the order that our Churches exhibit: that is, one man assuming to have *all* gifts in himself; but what we may call a constitutional monarchy, in which *elders*, or a senate, together with the people, had their share. The "angel," or head messenger of the Church." (Rev. ii.) "Elders" ordained "in every Church" (Acts xiv. 23), and acting with the head pastor.

Of these "elders," some, but not all, "laboured in the Word and teaching" (doctrine). (1 Tim. v. 17.) Then there were "exhorters," "deacons," and "evangelists" (or Gospel preachers), who were sent out by the Churches upon temporary missions. For each such mission the evangelist *may* have received the Church's blessing and "laying on of hands" for their special work. Thus were Saul and Barnabas commissioned by the Church of Antioch (Acts xiii. 3), though by all the Churches they had long before been acknowledged and accredited.

Such appears to have been the HOLY SPIRIT's "Church order." Each brother who had a "spiritual gift" (Rom. xii. 6) was to use that gift for the benefit of the world, or for "the edifying of the Church."

PART IV.

Scripture Testimony—continued.
The Epistles.

PART IV.

Scripture Testimony—continued.
The Epistles.

AND now to turn from the practice of Apostles as described in the "Acts," to the Apostles' doctrine as described in their Epistles. The latter are twenty-one in number, out of these Epistles three are devoted chiefly to the offices and work of *ministers of the Churches;* or, as they are called,—bishops, elders, evangelists, and deacons. Timotheus and Silas, to whom these Epistles are written, were sent to "set in order" the Churches which they visited. Their own personal holiness, their preaching of a true Gospel, and their constant service of love, are also much dwelt on. They were, for the time being, to preside over all ministers and Churches within the area of their visits. Out of the eighteen Epistles that remain, the two shorter letters of John are written to single Christians. The sixteen which remain, are written to "Churches." To the people then, or "laity," was the great bulk of Apostolic teachings addressed. All readers must be struck with this fact.

While then the Apostles' exhortations seem to be so centred on the people, on their faith and their obedience, their personal duties and obligations, have those people no share in *ministry* or in teaching of Divine truth? Let the two first apostolic Epistles answer this question. (Romans xii. chapter, and 1 Corinthians xii. chapter.) From Romans xii. it appears that the believers at Rome needed caution as to their thinking too highly of the "spiritual gifts" which they had received for the spiritual good of their brethren. Gifts these, not of money, nor what we call high learning and *education*, but gifts of spiritual knowledge, and of power to use that knowledge by the teaching and exhortation of others; in other words to use their *ministry*. "I say to *every man* that is among you (you are all interested in this matter), to think soberly, according as God hath dealt to *every man* the measure of faith. (Ver. 3.) Having then (all of you) gifts differing according to the grace given to us, whether prophecy, let us prophesy according to the proportion of faith (ver. 5); or ministry, let us wait on our ministering: or he that teacheth, on teaching (ver. 7); or he that exhorteth, on exhortation: he that giveth, let him do it with simplicity; he that ruleth, with

THE EPISTLES.

diligence; he that sheweth mercy, with cheerfulness." (Ver. 8.) In 1 Corinthians xii. we read: "To one is given by the Spirit the word of wisdom; to another the word of knowledge by the same Spirit; to another faith by the same Spirit; to another the gifts of healing; to another the working of miracles; to another prophecy; to another discerning of spirits; to another divers kinds of tongues; to another the interpretation of tongues." (Verses 8—10.) In verse twenty-eight of this chapter, we read, "God hath set some in the Church, first Apostles, secondarily Prophets, thirdly teachers; after that miracles, then gifts of healing, helps, governments, diversities of tongues."

From these seven "gifts" named in Romans xii., and the nine "gifts" in 1 Corinthians xii., we at once take away what are extraordinary and strictly *miraculous* "gifts." Healings, tongues, discernment of spirits, and prophecy in its highest sense we exclude. But there remain "ministry," "teaching," "exhortation," "giving" (or distributing), "ruling," and "showing mercy," "the word of knowlege," "the word of wisdom" and "faith." These nine "gifts" remain surely to the Church for all ages.

As to "ruling," it of course appertains to presiding ministers,—bishops, or elders. It has been also generally thought that "he that ministereth" ($\delta\iota\alpha\kappa o\nu\epsilon\iota$) refers to "ordained" ministers alone. The word "ministry" belongs however to all Christian service, —from the "ministry of the Word" by Apostles (Acts vi. 4), to Phœbe's, as διακονον or "deaconness," —"a *servant* of the Church." (Rom. xvi. 1.)

In St. Paul's preface to his list of the "gifts" (in 1 Cor. xii.), he says: "There are diversities of *administrations*." In the Greek it is, "differences of διακονιων—*ministries*." Upon this passage Dean Alford well remarks in his "Commentary," "These διακονιαι must not be narrowed to the *ecclesiastical* orders but kept commensurate in extent, with the gifts which are to find scope by their means." (See vol. ii.)

But "the word of wisdom," the "word of knowledge," with the powers of "exhortation" and "teaching," are not miraculous gifts. The power of "exhorting" and of "teaching," was to be used by each brother according to his "gift," for the "edifying of the Church." (1 Cor. xiv. 12.) We may indeed ask, To whom and where were brethren to address their "exhortations" except to their fellow-Christians in the Church assemblies, or to the ignorant and irreligious who were "*without*"? And if so, the people,—or laity, had their proper share and place in the "ministry of the Word." All doubt on this point must be removed by the Apostle's direction to all the Hebrew Christians: "Not forsaking *the assembling of ourselves together*, as the manner of some is: but exhorting one another: and so much the more, as ye see the day approaching." (Heb. x. 25.) Here are two directions to all the brethren: (1) assemble together; (2) exhort one another. What is an "assembling" of believers but a Church meeting? What is this mutual "exhortation" by brethren but a *ministry?* A *lay* ministry if we like to call it so.

One of the nine "gifts" common to the Church in all ages is doubtless here set forth. St. Paul's words would have no meaning for us, in these and all the many directions which he gave, if we might not "assemble together" and "exhort one another" in the Church meetings.

But how long have all these DIVINE words been neglected? It was Wesley who first sought to revive these primitive "assemblings" for mutual exhortation amongst believers. And such meetings tended greatly to cement the Methodist brethren in fellowship. Our "Church of England" still remains a complete blank as to such fellowship. A Church must be very far gone from apostolic practice, which, through its presiding ministers, makes no provision for these social meetings of believers.

Before leaving the testimony of St. Paul's two first Epistles, we must remark upon the large space which he gives to "prophesying" as an integral part of a Church's "*ministry.*" As regards its miraculous power—foretelling things to come,—or of "understanding all mysteries" (as it appears to mean in 1 Cor. xiii. 2), it cannot surely have been the "gift" which the Apostle so earnestly desired for all his brethren: "Covet earnestly the best gifts .... but ... rather that ye may prophecy." (1 Cor. xii. 31, and xiv. 1.)

In verse three we read that "He that prophesieth speaketh unto edification and *exhortation* and comfort." In Acts xv. 32 we also read that "Judas and Silas, being Prophets also, *exhorted* and comforted." Prophecy here seems to mean a speaking under a high elevation of DIVINE love, wisdom, and power in the heart, but short of what we call *immediate inspiration*. Speaking thus from a sanctified heart, and from an enlightened judgment, is a "gift" which has, I believe, never left the Church of CHRIST, and which will never leave it.

Having now seen St. Paul's teaching to the Churches of Rome and Corinth, let us look to the *practice* of those Churches as far as the Epistles throw light upon it.

If we turn to Philippians, chapter 1, we find St. Paul writing from Rome to his beloved converts at Philippi. This appears to have taken place during his first long imprisonment at Rome, about A.D. 61. For many previous years, however, the message of salvation had spread widely there, both amongst Jews and Gentiles. It had borne abundant fruit to the praise of GOD. (Rom. i. 8.) Large enough also had the body of believers become, to contain "divisions" amongst them. (Rom. xvi. 17.) St. Paul thus writes (verse 12 of chapter i.): "My bonds in CHRIST are become manifest in all the *palace*, and in all other places; and MANY OF THE BRETHREN, waxing confident through my bonds, are much more bold to speak the Word without fear; some indeed *preach* CHRIST even of envy and of strife, and some also of good will. The one preach CHRIST of contention, not sincerely, supposing to add affliction to my bonds; the other of love, knowing that I am set for the defence of the Gospel. What then? notwithstanding, every way CHRIST is preached," etc., etc.

A more accurate rendering of some important words in this Scripture will give greater force to the Apostle's meaning. (Verse 13.) "My bonds are made manifest that they are in CHRIST, throughout the *Prætorian* camp, and to all the rest:" *i.e.*, army.* (Verse 14.) "And *the greater part* of the brethren" (not many of the brethren," as in our version) "are much more bold to speak the Word without fear." (Verse 15.) "Some indeed *preach* CHRIST of envy," etc.

Here, then, are two great points established. (1)

* See Professor Lightfoot's admirable Commentary on these verses, and his elaborate explanation of the "Prætorion" erroneously translated "palace." Pp. 86 and 97 of his Work, second edition.)

The *greater part of the brethren* "spoke the Word with boldness." Considering the large number of believers in the Roman Church, and that the *greater part* of them " spoke the Word," we have to inquire *where* they used their gift. Was it merely in private Church meetings that they "spoke the Word"? Surely they needed not "*boldness*" for speaking the Word to one another. It must have been before the heathen Romans, or before those unbelieving Jews who so abounded in the city, that courage to speak the Word was necessary.

(2) But these brethren not only "*spoke* the Word;" they *preached* it. " Some of them *preach* CHRIST of envy," &c. The word is κηρυσσειν,—" *to proclaim, as an herald.*" Throughout the Gospels and the Acts this word is used to describe the preaching of our LORD and of HIS Apostles. Out of sixty-one Scriptures which contain the word κηρμσσω, fifty-five (in our English Bibles) render it *preach;* and in the six remaining Scriptures it is rendered "publish" and "proclaim," implying *public* teaching or proclaiming.

Most of the Roman brethren then had become *preachers;* bold preachers of Christ to those who were ignorant of His blessed Gospel.

The next questions that arise are : Did the Apostle, as the great ruler of Churches, approve this preaching? or did he declare it irregular and insubordinate, because he had not laid hands on nor commissioned the preachers? Did he order them to stop their preaching?

Let his own words answer: "What then? Every way .... CHRIST is preached. *I therein do rejoice; yea, and will rejoice.*"

The next question is, Were these brethren "preachers" *ordained* (as we use that term); that is to say, set apart for exclusive ministry, and ministry alone, so that they had to give up their usual worldly business, and cast themselves for support upon the Church's bounty? We have no intimation to that effect. St. Paul was a prisoner within the *Prætorian camp*, where were collected thousands of Imperial soldiers. As Prof. Lightfoot has reasonably argued, in his excellent work on the Philippians, the Apostle's chief intercourse, during his two years of imprisonment laid probably with Roman soldiers. Many, doubtless, of those brave men had watched his daily patience and meekness, and listened to his brotherly teaching; many doubtless believed, and turned to the LORD." Then there was "Cæsar's household," out of which many had become servants of CHRIST. In chapter iv. 22 (of Philipp.) we read, "All the Saints salute you, and chiefly they that are of "Cæsar's household." It appears that within the Emperor's "household" not only were slaves, and other attendants, but a great part of the city population,—all workmen and merchants, &c., who furnished anything towards the Emperor's wants or luxuries, were of his "household." We are not told that Cæsar's servants left his service because they turned to the Faith, and gave up idolatry. If, therefore, they kept on in his service, but went out occasionally to "preach Christ," they could not have been ordained, as *we* say, to a life of ministry. And it, therefore, follows that as simple unofficial "believers," they went forth to "preach." And though some of them had mixed and corrupt motives in so preaching, it was not their preaching which St. Paul condemned, it was their bad motives.

It is unnecessary to carry our search further into the Epistles. If Roman soldiers and workmen might and did "preach Christ," so might soldiers or workmen at Philippi, Ephesus, Colosse, or Thessalonica, do the same. Of the Philippian brethren in general, we read that they "*held forth* the Word of life." (Philipp. i.) Of the Colossians: "Let the word of Christ dwell in you richly in all wisdom; teaching and *admonishing* one another in psalms," etc. (Col. iii. 16—25.) To the Thessalonians it was written (1 Thess. v. 11), "Comfort: *i.e.*, *exhort one* another, and edify one another." "They were to warn them that are unruly, comfort the feeble-minded, support the weak...*Despise not prophesyings.*" Which seems to be a caution against despising those high "gifts" because the poorer brethren possessed them.

PART V.

The Ministry of Women.

PART V.

The Ministry of Women.

"Your conclusion, however, proves too much," it will be said. "Women, no doubt, formed part of the scattered multitude who preached. Did the women preach every where as well as the men? And if you maintain that the women preached, how does that consist with the plain command, 'Let your women keep silence in the Churches;' and, 'I suffer not a woman to teach.'" (1 Cor. xiv. 34; 1 Tim. ii. 12.)

Answer. Women, no doubt, formed a large part of the company. That they preached, or taught also, is a fair inference from the narrative. And if the inference be correct, that women preached at all, it only proves that women might and ought to take a modest part in speaking of their SAVIOUR to the ignorant, provided that they thereby neglected no home duties, and that some great special call to leave the beaten way invites them. By 1 Cor. xiv. 34, women are forbidden to speak "*in the Churches,*" or meetings for worship and teaching. But even this law is qualified by the same Epistle. In 1 Cor. xi. 5, women may there pray or "prophecy," as well as men, if their heads be "veiled." Our English translation in verse 10 of 1 Cor. xi. may here be explained to some readers who do not know Greek. "A woman must have *power* on her head." We understand from verse 5 the meaning of this term. "Every woman that prayeth or prophesieth with her head *uncovered (unveiled)*, dishonoureth her head."

However strong the general conviction be against women speaking or preaching publicly, yet still by no Christian Church is the precept fulfilled literally, that women should "keep silence" in Church meetings. By all Christian Churches women are allowed to join audibly in singing, as well as in liturgic prayers, where such are used. The obvious meaning of St. Paul's strong words in 1 Tim. ii. 11, 12, seems to be as follows: "They were not to contradict nor dispute with the elders and Bishops of the Church in public. When they prayed or prophesied, they were to be *veiled.* Such veiling was their ordinary custom, as it still is, in all Eastern countries. "Because of the *angels*" they were to be veiled.

Women were to be thus modestly attired. I do not attempt to decide whether by these "angels" be intended heavenly or earthly ministers. For my own part, I believe them to be the presiding ministers or bishops of the Church,—"angels," or "messengers," as they are termed in the seven Asiatic Churches. (Rev. ii., iii.) And why not in all Churches? Those who wish to see the different opinions which have been long held upon these "angels," will find them in Dean Alford's Commentary on 1 Cor. xi. 1, and in Pool's "Synopsis." But we must look at the whole evidence from the New Testament, direct and indirect, in order to gain a just view of the question of Women's Ministry.

I. *On the Day of Pentecost, the women who formed part of the Church's company, named before in Acts i. 14,* spoke by the SPIRIT's power, as well as did the men, "the wonderful works of GOD." (Ver. 11.) No exception is made: "They were *all* filled with the HOLY GHOST." (Ver. 4.) In explaining this miracle, Peter refers to Joel's prophecy. Joel had foretold, "Upon my servants (men) and upon my *handmaidens* will *I* pour out of MY SPIRIT *in those days, and they shall prophecy.*" (Ver. 18.) "Your sons and your *daughters* shall prophecy." (Ver. 17.) Here, then, at the very morning of the full Gospel-day, and of the "ministration of the SPIRIT" (2 Cor. iii. 8), were women called to "prophecy" in public.

It will be at once replied, "This prophesying was a miraculous gift, and limited to the first age. It is no precedent for women's preaching or teaching, either in Church meetings or in any public meeting." We grant that there is force in this answer. Nevertheless, according to 1 Cor. xiv. 1, "prophecying" is the gift which, above all others, believers are to "*covet after;*" because he that prophesieth, speaketh unto exhortation, and edification, or "building up," and "comfort," or "persuasion." Now it appears that to "exhort," to "build up," and to "comfort," have been gifts perpetually enjoyed amongst believers. In the Colossian Church (Colos. iii. 16), "Let the Word of CHRIST dwell in you richly in all wisdom; *teaching* and *admonishing* one another," etc. To the Roman believers (Rom. xv. 14), "Ye are full of goodness, filled with all knowledge, able also to *admonish one another.*" Such "exhortations" and "edifyings" as these do not surely imply a full, DIVINE, or infallible guidance. They rather imply that the speaker's heart and mind were filled with a holy and joyful possession of the truth which he would enforce upon others, and that he spoke from "the abundance of his heart" words which went with living power to the hearts of others. He was not, in the strict sense of that word, *inspired;* still the precept to all believers was, "If any man speak, let him *speak as the oracles of* GOD." (1 Pet. iv. 11.) And again, in Eph. v. 18, "Be ye filled with the SPIRIT." The man or woman who could thus "admonish" and "exhort," might be truly said, so far, to prophesy, or to speak under DIVINE influence, though they are left to their own choice of words, and their own arrangement of ideas and subjects.

One more Apostolic order brings out the duty of Christian women more distinctly addressing Jewish believers; I have already remarked upon it in the former chapter. St. Paul tells them, women as well as men, to *exhort one another* in companies or meetings (Heb. x. 25), "not forsaking the assembling of ourselves together . . . but *exhorting one another*. Unless, therefore, the Apostle limited this meeting together and this mutual exhorting, to men only, how can *we* do so? As well might we limit the precept, "Let us draw near with a true heart" (Heb. x. 22); or, "Let us hold fast the profession of our faith without wavering" (ver. 23); and if "assembling ourselves together" (ver. 24) refers to women as well as to men, then women were equally called on with men, according to their ability, to "exhort."

But we have more to say from SCRIPTURE. *The believers "scattered" after Stephen's martyrdom, and who "preached every where," included* women *as well as* men. If it be urged that women are not here named as preachers, we reply that the burden of proof lies on the objector, to show that women were not included in the "multitude;" and that if they were so included, they were *silent*. Such exclusion cannot, however, be proved. I therefore take the narrative in its plain, literal sense. I believe that when the mothers or wives of the scattered brethren fled with their husbands and children from Jerusalem, they spoke of the truth to women and children whom they met upon their journey. This may have been done without their standing up to address a mixed crowd: such would be their "preaching."

But let us see whether in the Epistles there be not some direct notice of, or allusion to, the preaching of women.

II. St. Paul, at a late period of his course, told the Philippians to "help *those women* who (had) laboured" with himself "in the *Gospel.*" (Phil. iv. 3.) Is it not plain that these women had a teaching ministry of some kind, however subordinate? The very word here translated "laboured" is συνηθλησαν,"—"*they joined in the contest*" of the Gospel,—gives the notion of some active work. We cannot hold with the opinion that it means only "they helped Paul to preach by helping him in his temporal wants." What he laboured in they laboured in: "they *laboured with me.*" *

---

* See Scheusner's Lexicon. The word means (1) "to exercise oneself *with* others in the *Gymnasium* (school of contests); (2) metaphorically "to join in a common labour, diligently, and by all means, to help another who is labouring." The word only occurs twice in the New Testament, and both times in this Epistle to Philippians,—*here*, and in *Phil.* i. 27. In the latter

The women here spoken of appear to be Euodia and Syntyche, just before named. Our ablest present Commentators (Bishop Ellicott, Dr. Lightfoot, and Dean Alford) consider that the whole passage thus means: "I beseech Euodia and Syntyche that they be of one mind. Help these women (to be of one mind), inasmuch as they *laboured* in the Gospel,"—"the message of good news,"—as this word invariably means. These women had laboured in the *delivery of that message*. Read also the words that follow: "Those women who *strove together* in the Gospel, with Clement, and with other my fellow-labourers."

Does any one doubt that Clement was a real fellow-*preacher* of the Gospel with Paul? But Paul joins the women and Clement together. All three were fellow-labourers with himself "*in the Gospel.*" What can be plainer than that these women were in some way or other *preachers* or *teachers* of the Gospel? It may have been that the Apostle employed them to teach women only, but *that* was Gospel work.

In Rom. xvi. and Phil. iv., we have several

---

text our version has it, "*Striving together* for the faith of the Gospel." Our translators have rendered the word more correctly, "*Striving* together for the faith;" or, rather, "in the faith of the Gospel." As well, then, might the word have been translated in Phil. iv. 3, "Help those women who have *striven* with me in the Gospel." Were our translators afraid of giving thereby countenance to *female* ministry?

women named by St. Paul as taking some part in the Gospel ministry: I mean of the ministry of teaching. We see in Rom. xvi. 1, "Phebe, a *servant* of the Church in Cenchrea." The former translators of our English Bible here render the Greek word διακονον (diaconon) "*servant* of the Church." But why give this word a different meaning from what they have given it in 1 Tim. iii. and Phil. i. 1? There treating of two orders of ministers, the Apostle calls the second order, διακονοε (diaconoi). Our translators here render it "*deacons.*" Why, then, is not Phœbe here termed a *female minister*, or a "deaconness"? Our translators appear to have shrunk from acknowledging the *teaching* ministry of women. Nevertheless, here and elsewhere, are many women honoured by the Apostle as *deaconesses*. In Rom. xvi. 3, "Salute Prisca, or Priscilla." (See Acts xviii. 2.) She, with Aquilla her husband, "expounded to Apollos the way (of truth) more perfectly." Here, then, at least, was a woman employed to teach a man,—one, too, who was "mighty in the Scriptures," and afterwards a most successful preacher. (1 Cor. iv. 5. Acts xviii. 24.) And when it is added that "all the Churches of the Gentiles give thanks" to Priscilla as well as to Aquilla, we may fairly doubt whether *her* ministry was confined only to helping poor believers with food, clothing, and *nursing;* and whether she who could explain the "way of life" to Apollos the eloquent, did not explain it to *hundreds*, whether in smaller or larger companies. Five other women are then named: Mariam (Rom. xvi. 6), Junia (ver. 7), "Tryphena and Tryphosa" (ver. 12), and "the beloved Persis." Rufus's "mother" and Nereus's "sister" are then named. Three of these women are said to "labour in the LORD," and JUNIA to have been "of note among the Apostles." (Ver. 7.) What their precise labours were we are not told; but in Phil. iv. 2, we read that two other women, Euodia and Syntyche, had "laboured in the Gospel."*

We fully admit that *preaching*, in the general meaning and acceptation of that term, is not enjoined on women. It is on occasions of extraordinary necessity, as we say, that their ministry, on a public scale, might be called for; but, assuredly, *we* have "extraordinary necessity" in the present state of our great city populations. To this I will afterwards refer.

Let us now note some signal marks of DIVINE favour on the ministry of women, as recorded in SCRIPTURE.

First, then, who would forget that an outcast *woman* was once the most successful herald of our adorable LORD? "The *woman* left her waterpot, and

---

* Our translators have here mistaken in putting Euodias (masculine) instead of a woman's name of Euodia.

went her way into the city, and saith to the MEN
("daring irregularity," as we might say), Come, see
a man, who told me all things that ever I did: is
not this the CHRIST?" (John iv. 28, 29.) Remark
here, this Samaritan had not been *told* by her LORD
to make HIM thus publicly known. "Go, call thy
husband, and come hither" (ver. 16), was the order
given. But her trusting heart must tell out somehow
the glad tidings. Whatever we choose to call it,—
whether she spoke in the middle of the street of
Sychar, or whether she called her neighbours to her
house, she *told* them what she had seen and heard.
She *told* all with word and action so really, that all
the men "went out of the city, and came unto HIM."
(Verse 31.) We may fairly suppose that the term
"men" may here include all the people in general,
as in Acts iv. 4. But were her hearers only *men*, her
boldness, as an eastern woman, was almost incredible.
The point however for our consideration is, Did our
gracious LORD reprove her for it? Did HE say,
"Women are for ever forbidden to speak of ME in
an assembly, or to give help in bringing precious
souls nearer to MYSELF"? No hint have we of such
a forbidding. But not only so,—GOD'S SPIRIT honoured
her word, and made it to lead sinners to believe on
HIMSELF. "*Now* we *believe*," they said to the woman:
"not because of thy saying; but we have heard HIM
ourselves, and believe that this is indeed the CHRIST,

the Saviour of the world." (Verse 42.) Many Samaritans had, it thus appears, believed on Him first through the woman's testimony; but a multitude more were led, through her simple testimony, to go to Him, to inquire, and to *believe*. Such success as this did not attend the first preaching by the "seventy," as far as we may judge of its effects from Luke x. 17: "Even the *devils* are subject unto us through Thy name," the seventy replied. But they could not say that "men," more hard to be convinced than were lost spirits, had repented or believed the Gospel. The Lord Jesus might have sent ten out of the "seventy" disciples, or two out of the twelve Apostles, in order to announce to the Samaritans that He was at Jacob's well, and that He waited there to give unto them "living water." But He was pleased to use this woman's ministry to do a work which Apostles did not and might not do; for "into any city of the Samaritans" they were not to enter. (Matt. x. 5.) How soul-refreshing is it to see the woman daring thus to act in her Maker's presence! to do what she dared not do merely before man! Her soul, like an uncaged bird, has burst the bars of fear. It soars and sings " in the open firmament of heaven."

And lastly, to whom was He pleased *first* to reveal Himself after His resurrection? Whom did He make the first herald of that all-glorious event,

—a herald of it, not to women only, but to men also,—even to "Apostles whom HE had chosen"? "HE appeared *first* to Mary Magdalene, out of whom HE had "cast seven devils" (Mark xvi. 9); and said to her, "Go to my *brethren*, and say unto them, I ascend to MY FATHER," etc. Such was HIS command. (John xx. 17.) But St. Matthew tells us of a double commission given to Mary and to "the other women" named as joining her after she had left the Garden (John xx. 10), (1) by the angel who had rolled away the stone from the sepulchre. (Matt. xxviii. 5—7.) "Go quickly and tell HIS disciples that HE is risen." (2) By the LORD HIMSELF. (Verse 9.) "And as they" (the women) "went to tell HIS disciples, behold, JESUS met them. Then said JESUS unto them, Be not afraid: go tell my brethren that they go before ME into Galilee." (Matt. xxviii.)

What can we say to these things? Who can doubt that as HE was pleased, after that great event, to make these women the first messengers of HIS finished work on earth, so it may please HIM, and has pleased HIM, to choose women, since HIS Ascension, to speak to others of HIS finished work of mediation in heaven? What, then, are such *special* times for women's special ministry, but the times in *which we live?* Are not women's loving hearts and words wanted to speak of Salvation amidst the *million and half* of grown up people in London, who are living and dying in sin? or to the 300,000 neglected souls in Manchester? What shall we say of the modest but impressive teaching of the late Mrs. Stevens (of Knowesborough)? How many hearts and consciences did her *preaching* arrest, as she spoke from her chair at the good Vicar's schoolroom? *Three Bishops* were sometimes amongst her listeners; and one of our most distinguished Deans has avowed that his conversion to the living Power of the Gospel, flowed from her teaching?

What shall we say of the beloved Mrs. Daniells, lately passed from her earthly ministry? Her life's last years, her money, her prayers, her voice were spent in bringing the Gospel of the Resurrection amongst our army at Aldershott camp. She taught it herself—as well as helped many others to teach it —to soldiers themselves as well as to soldiers' wives.

And what shall we say of the many Christian women who, in our times, have "laboured in the Gospel"? What of Elizabeth Fry, the angel friend of female prisoners? What bishop, clergyman, or dissenting minister, had power or spiritual gifts that could win the sin-hardened convict women in Newgate prison? When her silver voice calmed the furious into attention; when her benign look helped her words, was she an authorized *Evangelist* or messenger of good? Surely we need not ask such questions. She reasoned with, she "exhorted," she intreated the prisoners to flee from coming wrath; to look unto JESUS; to be reconciled to GOD. Was this to *preach?* However we may term it, and explain it away, there was her DIVINE call to minister,—there was she manifestly raised up to set an example to that class so much to be pitied in our community,—the class of *highly refined and educated ladies;* to show to those "ladies" what Christian women should be, and what they should *do* for the most degraded of their own sex.

But what is the general state of our lady class, whose mission it should be to work for a Saviour's glory, by the teaching of women and children and by helping onward their earthly as well as their eternal good? Amongst us there are many cases of noble female devotion to holy service. But *in general,* what are the thousands spent by our Christian ladies upon "*dress*" and personal ornaments? What thousands do they spend in the teaching of what are commonly called "accomplishments" to their daughters? How many in order to "introduce" them into society, to get them *admired,* and to enable them to make *good* (*i.e.,* good worldly) marriages? How great must be the change in our *lady class* before it can fulfil its heavenly mission!

Let them hear the Apostle speak: " Whose adorning let it not be that outward (adorning) of plaiting the hair, or of wearing of gold, or of putting on of apparel." (1 Pet. iii. 3.) What would the Apostle have said of the *bare faced* look of our women?

Our conclusion then from this comparison of New Testament Scripture is, That women had, and ought to have, their proper place of ministry, both in teaching and evangelizing. That St. Paul's two prohibitions in 1 Tim. ii. and 1 Cor. xiv., cannot be reasonably pressed so as to discourage and forbid *all* such ministry. That the bishops and pastors of churches ought to regulate and encourage such ministry, and not to despise or disparage it; but to cherish every effort, that the godly women in their Churches would put forth for the good of souls. That bishops and pastors ought to commission and set apart godly women for this work; that there are special occasions of urgent necessity which will justify the taking of a more public part in ministry by women than would be otherwise required; and that such special necessity for women's ministry exists to a large degree in England and Scotland at the present day, when whole masses of people in our large towns are still unevangelized.

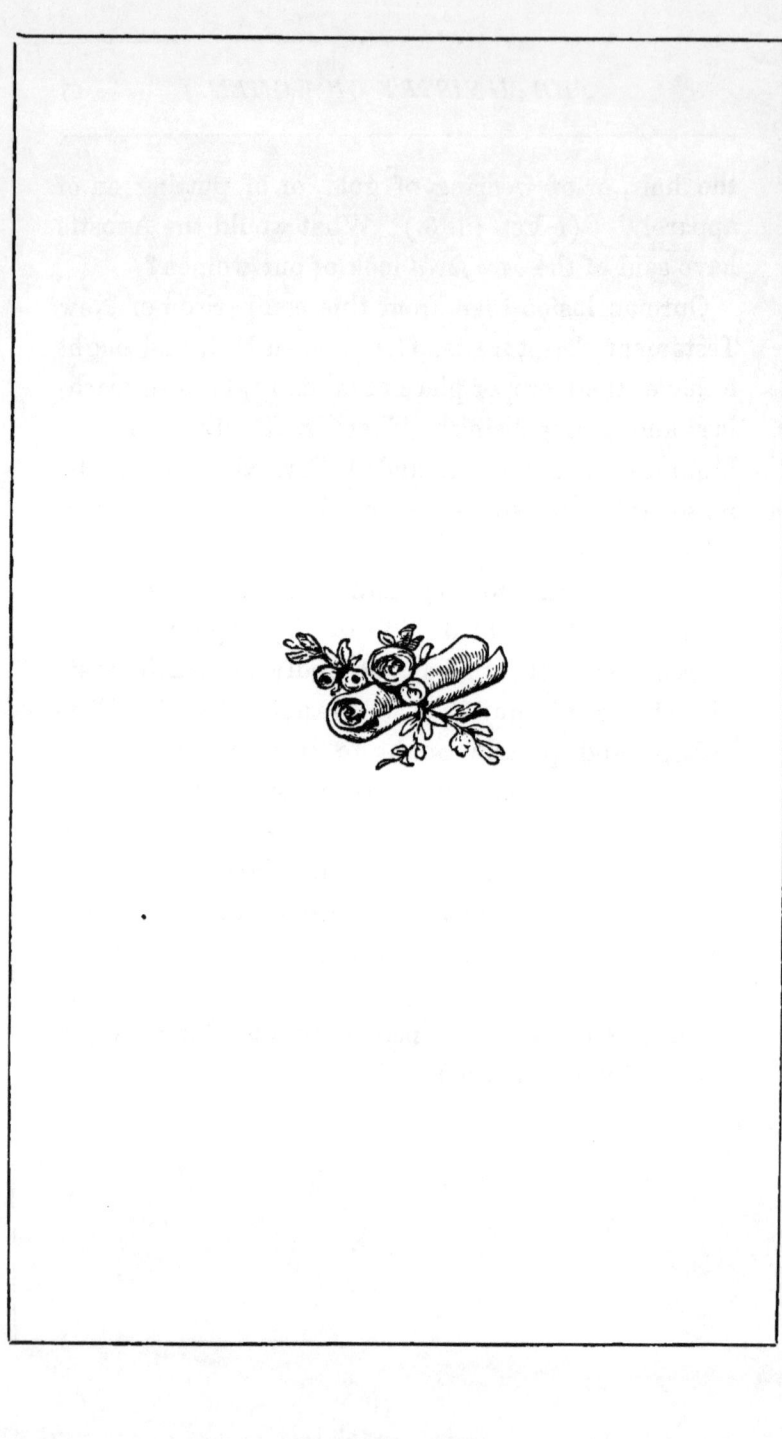

PART VI.

(I.)

*The Reasons why
Lay Preaching and Teaching fell into
Disuse. Ministerial Rank.*

PART VI.

The Reasons why Lay Preaching and Teaching fell into Disuse. Ministerial Rank.

WE have now established the fact that during the Apostles' times, *unordained* men, and women also, held an important place in the ministry of the Gospel. We have seen that "evangelists" were appointed by the LORD to a ministry distinct in itself, though that ministry might be to some extent combined with that of *pastor* and Bishop. We may now inquire how it was that this lay-evangelism fell into disuse, and how it became at last forbidden. We need not take a long time to explain it. The Bishops and pastors of churches became by degrees invested with unscriptural honour and dignity, and were at last deemed to be PRIESTS, in the literal and proper sense of that term: viz., a Jewish sacrificing priest.

(1) *Unscriptural honours and dignities began very early to be heaped on the head Bishops of Churches.* We

may give here a few illustrations of this fact out of Bingham's learned book on "Christian Antiquities." It is not that we grudge any due or decorous respect to the "rulers" of the Churches. Where such respect is denied to them something must be wanting in ourselves by too lowered a view of the ministerial calling. But this respect is due not to *office*, or names of rank which men may heap on ministers, but to their earnest piety and diligent labours. "Know them who are over you in the LORD. Esteem them very highly in love for their work's sake." (1 Thess. v. 12, 13.) "Remember them that have the rule over you, who *have spoken to you the Word of* GOD." (Heb. xiii. 7.) All such respect, however, is totally different from giving to them the worldly honour of great names, great wealth, and elevated seats and thrones, and the ascription of power such as the LORD JESUS did not bestow upon His Apostles.

Turn to Bingham (book ii., ch. 2), upon the titles and dignities to which Bishops were gradually advanced: "Princes," or "chiefs" of the people (p. 69); "Chiefs of the *priests*" (*Sacerdotum*, the Jewish priest); and "Great High Priest" (*Pontifex Maximus*, the title of the *heathen Roman high priest*, taken into the Christian Church) (p. 71); "Every Bishop anciently called Father, Papa, or Pope" (p. 72); "Father of Fathers and Bishop of Bishops" (p. 74); "Patriarchs" (p. 7); "Vicars of CHRIST" (p. 78). Then, in ch. ix., on "the

FELL INTO DISUSE. 73

honours paid to Bishops": "Bending the head, to receive their blessing" (p. 127); "Kissing their hands" (p. 128); "Singing hosannas to them sometimes, but not approved" (p. 129); "Saluting Bishops *per coronun*" (p. 130). Bishops are to be called "most dear to GOD most holy" (p. 133). Then come the titles of "Archbishops," "Primates," and "Patriarchs," in an ascending scale of dignity, till at last the Roman Bishop claimed dominion over the Universal Church, and obtained it through the Western Roman Empire, under Justinian. (A.D. 533.)

What would the Apostle Peter have said to Christians who would bend down for his episcopal "benediction," or crave his "absolution"? "Stand up," would he not have said, as he did to Cornelius, "for I also am a man"? (Acts x. 22.)

Bingham tells us that by the third century, presbyters (elders) were not permitted to sit down in the presence of "the Bishop." On the same principle, Mosheim informs us that "*sub-deacons*" might not sit down in the presence of a "deacon." (Mosheim, cen. iii., part iii., ch. ii., vol. i., p. 238. Notes. Edit., 1826.)

We find also that by the third century there were four degrees of rank set up in the higher clergy, and six degrees amongst what were called "the minor orders" (Mosheim, p. 239): deacons, sub-deacons, exorcists, readers, attendants (acolyths), and doorkeepers. (See also Neander's "Church History," vol. i., pp. 238, 239.) But we find no order of "*evangelists*" named in these lists. We hear of no laymen who might have gifts for preaching the Gospel, encouraged and authorized to do so, and commissioned by the Bishop or elders of a Church to evangelize the ignorant.

Finally, to illustrate the unapostolic and exaggerated honour paid to "the Bishop," let us take the testimony of one early Church writer during the second century. IGNATIUS, Bishop of Antioch, and a martyr for the faith, wrote epistles to many of the Churches in Asia Minor. That these epistles in their original form were very early interpreted by subsequent writers, there can be no doubt. Learned men have given us the choice of two texts in which to read Ignatius. Both of these texts, however, cannot be genuine. From the shorter of them, which perhaps bears the strongest evidence of genuineness, I cite the following statements about "Bishops." Epistle to Ephesians, ch. vi.: "It is manifest, therefore, that we should look upon the Bishop as on CHRIST HIMSELF." Epistle to Magnesians, ch. vi.: "Your Bishop presides *in the place of* GOD." To the Trallians, ch. iii.: "In like manner, let us reverence the *deacons* as an appointment of JESUS CHRIST, and the Bishops as JESUS CHRIST." To the Smyrnæan Church, ch. ix.: "It is well to reverence both GOD and the Bishop.

MINISTERIAL RANK. 75

He who honours the Bishop, has been honoured by
GOD. He who does anything *without the knowledge of
the Bishop, does serve the devil.*"
I make these quotations from the newest English
version of Ignatius' letters. ("Apostolic Fathers,"
translated by Roberts, Donaldson, and Crombie.
Ed. 1867.) This work places before us the larger
and the shorter texts. But how are we, as ordinary
scholars and students, to decide their merits? In his
masterly work upon Paul's Epistle to the Philippians,
Prof. Lightfoot says that the *shorter* version of Ignatius
"is probably corrupt or spurious." (Lightfoot on
Philippians, p. 242, in the "Dissertation on the
Christian Ministry.") Who is to decide?

If such views as these about Bishops were common
in Ignatius' time, how far had men travelled from "the
simplicity in CHRIST": "Not as though we had *dominion*
over your faith, but as being helpers of your joy."
(2 Cor. i. 24.) No wonder that the *people*, or *laity*,
began to sink in importance, in proportion as
"Bishops" and "elders" were raised to dignity half
DIVINE. How soon had the "fine gold" of the day
of Pentecost, and of the first Apostolic Churches,
"become dim"!

How short a time had the LORD's warning remained
with those who bore His name (Luke xxii. 24, 25):
"There was also a strife among them, which should
be accounted the greatest.... But he that is greatest

among you, let him be as the younger; and he that is chief, as he that doth serve." It is quite true that high titles and pride do not necessarily go together, no more than does humility follow men of lowest rank. But the many distictions of rank and respect set a worldly object of desire before the mind. CHRIST had said, "Call no man your Father (spiritually) on earth." The Church said, "Call your Bishops Fathers, Papæ, or *Popes*." It is natural to say, "How could Ignatius, a holy man, one who had seen and heard Apostles teach,—how could he thus write about Bishops, etc.? As a good man, he would never have *invented* such titles. Surely he must have had the Apostle's sanction for what he taught, as in the case of infant baptism. That practice, though not distinctly *ordered* by the Apostles, was permitted by them, or it never could have so generally and so early prevailed. So (may we not reason?) the duty of complete *submission to a presiding Bishop* by all the members of each Church, must have been sanctioned, if not directly ordered, by Apostles."

To all this we answer, where we find such difference of doctrine between that of the pupil and that of his Master, however good and holy the pupil was, we must cleave to the Master's teaching. The Apostles were teachers fully inspired by GOD, when they wrote their Epistles to the Churches. Not so inspired were Clement, Polycarp, or Ignatius, in writing their epistles.

Where, therefore, the inspired and uninspired so clash against and contradict each other, we have no choice left. We go to the spring, at its pure fountainhead. A few yards lower down, this stream may be losing its brightness amidst the mud and weeds of men's traditions. And so it undoubtedly did in this case.

Besides this, Peter, the Primate of the Apostles, when left to follow his own will in his *teaching*, taught grave error. He, when uninspired, would have put the Gentile converts under a half Jewish yoke. Paul is inspired to declare that Peter, with Barnabas and others, "walked not uprightly according to the truth of the Gospel." Paul "withstood Peter to the face, because he was to be blamed." (Gal. ii. 11.) Can we then be surprised that Ignatius, an uninspired teacher, should fall into some favourite notion about episcopal power, and think he was promoting true unity in the Churches by making the "Bishop" the centre of all spiritual light, around which the people were to revolve, and from which they were to draw their light? However honest he may have been, he can be no guide to us, if he departs from "the truth of the Gospel," as did Peter; and though Ignatius' doctrine about single Bishops became so soon afterwards generally received, we have only St. Paul's example to follow as to the standard by which to judge all things. The Gospel, as delivered by

Peter himself at Pentecost, and the Church order and discipline set up by Peter and his fellow-Apostles, are the Gospel and Church order by which we must test all subsequent teaching and all subsequent Church order.

Ignatius' doctrine, indeed, confutes itself. "*Do nothing apart from the Bishop.*" Had he seen what came to pass in the fourth century, he would have seen half the Bishops turn Arians. Would he then have taught, "Do nothing without your Arian bishop"? *i.e.*, "become Arians yourselves." Ignatius should have said, "Follow your Bishop as far as he follows the Gospel."

The "Bishops and deacons" with whom Paul was contented to correspond at Philippi, and the elders of Ephesus whom he called Bishops, or "overseers" (Acts xx. 28; Phil. i. 1), had now given way. The "Bishops and deacons" whom Timotheus and Titus were instructed to appoint "in every city," were no longer deemed sufficient rulers and ministers of the Churches.

One more of what are called "Apostolic Fathers," we may cite in order to show how early error came in to mar the real apostolic ministry. Clement of Rome comes second in the order of "Fathers." He may have been St. Paul's "fellow-labourer," as named in Phil. iv. 3. Tradition makes him the first presiding "Bishop" of the Roman Churches. We have remaining his two letters to the "Corinthian Christians."* They are considered to be genuine. It appears from Clement's first epistle, that these Corinthians had turned from the ministry of certain presbyters (elders) or pastors, whom an Apostle or his delegate had appointed or "ordained." (Acts xiv. See also ch. xl. of Clement's first epistle.) It is quite plain to any common reader of Clement, that his paramount object is to demand greater respect for and obedience to their appointed pastors. All the blessings which a Church might expect from GOD, seem in Clement's view to hang on this one thing. We may agree with Clement as to the sin and danger of a people casting off godly pastors who had truly "spoken to them the Word of GOD," and lived holy lives before them. But Clement's teaching in this matter is too unreserved. It is extravagant and unreasoning. What if the pastors should teach "another Gospel"?—should, like Peter, mix false doctrine with the truth? Were the Corinthians to submit to such error? Such was not Paul's doctrine. When Paul bade farewell to the Ephesian "elders" (Acts xx.), he foretold that some "from amongst themselves" would prove to be "wolves," not sparing the flock, "speaking *perverse things.*" (Ver. 29, 30.)

* See "Apostolic Fathers," as above cited. Also Archbishop Ware's translation of their writings, and the Rev. S. Chevallier's translation.

Clement, in order to justify this rash teaching, tells the Corinthians that ministerial *order* and ministerial precedence should prevail under the Gospel as well as under the Mosaic law. His words are in ch. xli. Speaking of ministerial offices, he says, "To the chief priest his peculiar offices are given, and to the priests their own place is appointed, and the layman (ὁ λαικορ) is confined within the limits of what is common to laymen."

Without openly avowing it, Clement seems to make "Bishops" and pastors take the place of the Jewish high priest, and the priests under him. And since high priest and priests under the law fell into their offices through family succession, and not by merit of personal holiness, so we suppose Clement to imply that Bishops and pastors were to be followed and obeyed, whether fit or unfit for their office.

"But the *layman* is confined within the limits of what *is common to laymen*." But what are the layman's limits? Clement does not tell us. He leaves us under the impression that the *laity*, that is, all the believers who were not regularly appointed ministers, had no ministry at all. How different such teaching from that of his own teacher, Paul!

St. Paul, as we have seen, had like Clement, written two letters to these same Corinthians, perhaps thirty years before. When Paul wrote, he had to blame them as much for over-valuing as under-

valuing their appointed teachers. "Who then is
Paul, and who Apollos, but ministers through whom
ye believed," etc.? But we read of no unquestioning,
unconditional obedience even to himself: "Let a man
so account of us (Apollos and himself, 1 Cor. iv. 6),
as the ministers of CHRIST, and stewards of the
mysteries of GOD." (1 Cor. iv. 1.) He tells them,
"Be followers of me, as I am also of CHRIST"
(1 Cor. xi.), but no further. If he corrupted the
Truth, they must flee from him. "Though we or
an angel from heaven preach any other Gospel than
that which ye have received, let him be *accursed.*"
(Gal. i. 8.)

As to our *submission to godly pastors*, it is a duty
which the Apostle in several places solemnly enjoins.
But in his first Epistle to Corinth, he extends this
submission to *all who in any way ministered*, according
to the various forms of ministry which the Apostle
enumerates. In 1 Cor. xvi. 15, 16, he says, "Ye know
the house (or family) of Stephanus, that they have
addicted themselves to the ministry of the saints;
*that ye submit yourselves to such, and to every one that
helpeth with us, and laboureth."* Here submission is
enjoined to a whole godly family, and to all earnest
"labourers in the Gospel;" and we have already
seen that *women* were amongst these fellow-labourers.
This is doctrine very different from that of Clement:
viz., *prostrate obedience to one set of ministers only;*

very different to that of Ignatius, who taught prostrate, blind obedience to one head minister.

Paul's delight it was to see all the brethren using their spiritual gifts, provided that they used them to edification. As to *office*, or personal dignity, he has said next to nothing. In one place, indeed, he said to the Corinthians, "I magnify mine office." (Rom. xi. 13.) But how did he magnify it?—"In all things approving *ourselves as* CHRIST'S *ministers*." (2 Cor. v. 6.) Surely, had implicit submission to any one pastor or Bishop been in St. Paul's view the standing remedy for a Church's divisions and disorders, St. Paul would at once have said so. When detained a prisoner at Rome, and when many brethren (as we have seen) disowned his apostolic teaching, could he not have told them, on DIVINE authority, that they must bow down to himself? But he rests all his claims to their allegiance to the unspotted purity of his life, to his extraordinary labours and sufferings for the good of their souls, and to the miraculous calling by which the "ministry" had been conferred upon him, "to testify the Gospel of the grace of GOD." No warrant did he leave for the teaching which our fathers and ourselves have so long heard: *i.e., reverence to Bishops and clergymen on account of their office*, and irrespective of their piety or spiritual gifts. As "successors of the Apostles" we have been told to regard all *ordained Bishops and clergy*. We

MINISTERIAL RANK. 83

have been told to believe a falsehood. Through mere "ordination," they never received "a spiritual gift" which they had not received before such ordination. *Ordination* is only the recognition of gifts and grace that have been bestowed on the ordained man *before* his ordination. Ordination is the outward commission which the ministers of a Church give to those who have been already "moved by the HOLY GHOST" to enter the ministry.

According to the Prayer-book Service for "Ordination," every candidate is supposed to have received some high "spiritual gift" for ministry, before he can honestly answer to the tremendous questions which are put to him by a Bishop, respecting his present holy standing in the faith of CHRIST, and his purpose of unreserved devotion to HIS Service. Had this Service consisted only of these questions, of prayer, exhortation, the answers, and the "laying on of hands," it had been well. But unfortunately the Bishop's hands are made to be the certain channel of the HOLY SPIRIT's Gifts. Of this error we must more fully speak in the next part. This error has caused nearly all the convulsion which is now heaving our National Church. Its only cure lies in its removal from the Prayer-book.

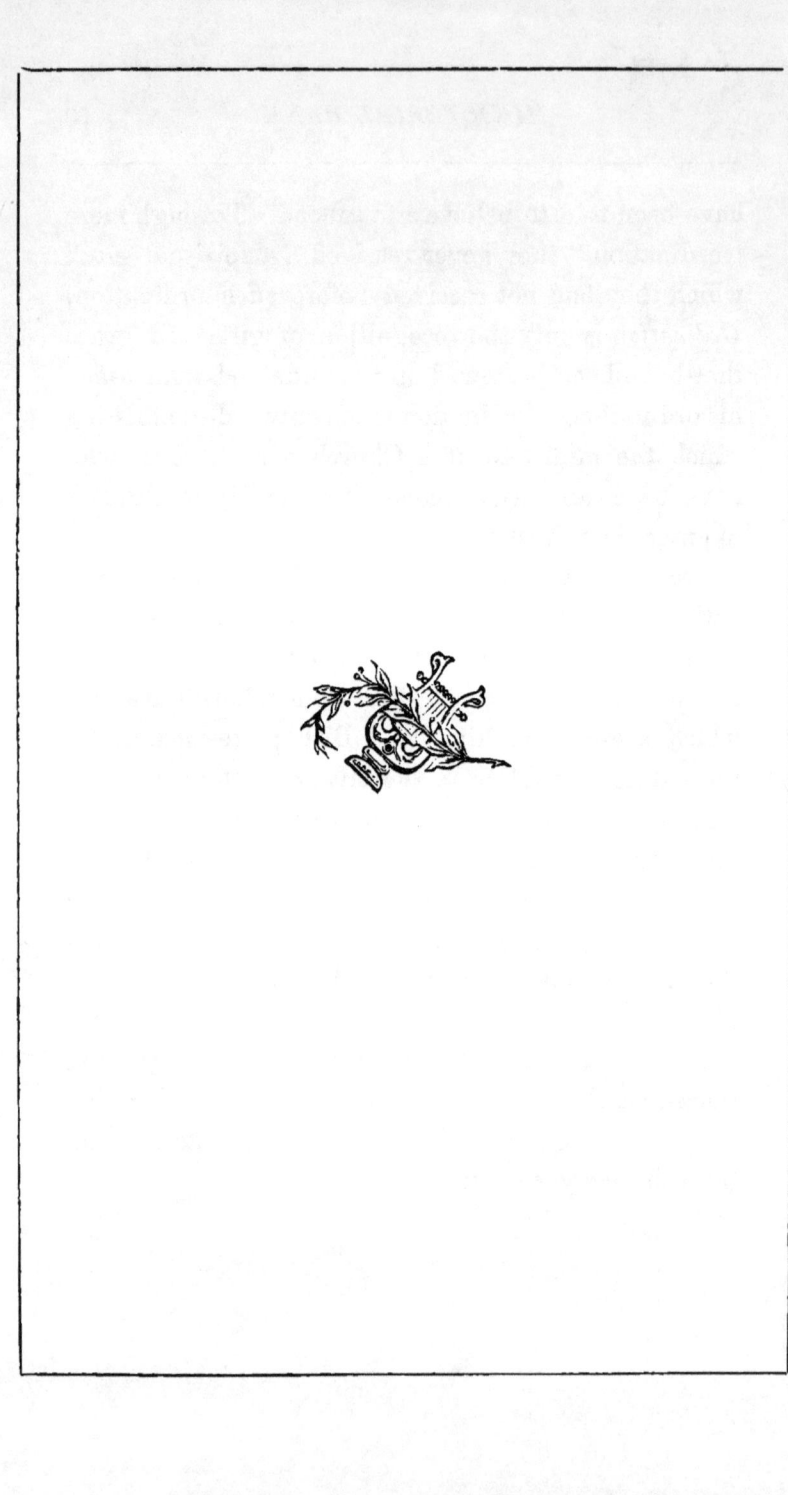

PART VI.

(II.)

Causes which Led to Stop Lay Ministry.
Priesthood.
Remains of Priesthood in the Church of England.

PART VI.

Causes which Led to Stop Lay Ministry. Priesthood.

Remains of Priesthood in the Church of England.

A FAR graver error than this unscriptural *dignity* of Bishops, soon arose. Bishops and pastors begun to be called and regarded as PRIESTS, and afterwards as *sacrificing* priests, like the Jewish or heathen priests. It is probable that nearly to the end of the second century, Bishops and pastors may have been called "priests," because they in a measure *represented* the people in the common prayer and praise of a Church meeting. They as it were offered up the "spiritual sacrifices" of devotion, as the mouthpiece of the brethren. Just so, in *our* Church meetings, ministers say, "*We* pray, *we* praise," as if they spoke in behalf of the congregation.

In order to show the progress of this error, we may turn again to Clement of Rome. He speaks of as we have seen, the "high priest," and the "priests." under him, apparently as fulfilling under the Law, what "Bishops and deacons" do under the Gospel. But in ch. xlvii. of his first letter to Corinth, his English translators have made Clement to call such ministers *priests*. Archbishop Wake, and the Rev. T. Chevallier, in their translation from the Greek, have done this. "It is dreadful, beloved, that the most firm and ancient Church of the Corinthians, should, by one or two persons, be led into a schism against their *priests*." (See also ch. xlv.) I cite these words from two translations of Clement's letters by Archbishop Wake, and by the late Rev. T. Chevallier.

It is surprising that two scholars, Archbishop Wake and Chevallier, should so mistranslate the word used by Clement. πρεσβύτερος, *presbyter*, is the word that Clement uses. By these scholars it was well known that in all the New Testament Scriptures where it occurs, it is never translated *priest*. The word invariably used is "*elders*." It occurs sixty-six times in the New Testament. Out of this number, sixty-five texts give the rendering "elder." Once only is it translated "old men" (in Acts ii.); and once (incorrectly) "eldest" (in Luke xvi.). The Greek word for "priest" is a word totally different. It is ἱερεύς. And to show how unfair and absurd, as well as dangerous to truth's cause it was thus wrongly to translate Clement's "presbyters," we may say that if Clement's elders may be called *priests*, so may the "elders" of the Jewish Church who are so

PRIESTHOOD. 89

often joined with the "chief priests" in the Gospel history, be translated "priests" also. Thus we should read in Matt. xxvii. 1, "All the chief priests and the *priests* of the people took counsel together."

But though Clement does not actually call pastors by a Jewish name, he is the first to suggest a resemblance between Levitical priests and Christian Bishops and ministers, if indeed he did not mean that Levitical priests were types of Gospel ministers. In his first letter (ch. xl. and xli.), Clement so presses his analogy of the old temple ritual, as a model for Christian Church-order, that few could doubt that in *his* view, the Gospel ministry was to be a successor of the Levitical priesthood. I subjoin his words (in ch. xl. and xli.): "We perform our *offerings* and service to GOD, at their appointed seasons. For these He hath commanded to be done, not rashly and disreally, but at certain determinate seasons and hours. He hath Himself ordained, by His supreme will, both where and by what person they are to be performed, that all things being piously done unto all well-pleasing, they may be acceptable to His will. They, therefore, who make their *oblations* at the appointed seasons, are accepted and happy; for they sin not, inasmuch as they obey the commandments of the LORD. For to the *chief priest* his peculiar offices are given, their own place is appointed; and to the *Levites* appertaining their proper ministries; and the *layman* is confined within the bounds of what is commanded to laymen."

Here remark (1) the rigid enforcement of "seasons" and "times" is just what St. Paul had before condemned and forbidden in the Galatian Church: "Ye observe days, and months, and times, and years; I am afraid of you, lest I have bestowed on you labour in vain." It was the return to Judaism. (2) Clement calls this Judaic "order" a DIVINE command to Christians. He says (ch. xl.), "These hath He commanded to be done at certain commanded times and hours." Against all this comes in the DIVINE warning (Matt. xv. 6), "Ye have made the Word of GOD of none effect by your tradition." (3) The *layman* is a newly-invented name for those who are uniformly called by the Apostles "brethren," "believers," "saints." We do not object to the distinction between people, or "laity," and ministers, elders, etc. But Clement's "layman" is actually put in contrast with the priest, and tends to sever the people of a Church from their universal *priesthood.**

---

* See Chevallier's note on ὁ λαικος ανηρ, page 40 of his "Apostolic Fathers." Any reader who wishes for a short and clear account of the gradual passage made from this universal priesthood (the calling of all believers), back to the Jewish or *Aaronic* priesthood, which Bishops and elders afterwards assumed, will do well to study Prof. Lightfoot's admirable "Dissertation on the Christian Ministry." It is appended to his notes upon St. Paul's Epistle to the Philippians.

Clement is no safe or dependable guide. He had left the *Pauline* standard. But to the grand error let us turn,—*that of a sacrificing, or sin-atoning priesthood*, of which Clement and other early writers sowed the seed. If human words can ever convey truth in a simple form, and if the HOLY SPIRIT deigns to teach truth to man through such human words, then the one great truth taught by that SPIRIT in the Epistle to the Hebrews, cannot be mistaken: "*That the* LORD JESUS *should offer up* HIMSELF *once, and once for all, to bear man's iniquity, and bear it away.*" The sacrifice of CHRIST was to be once only,—just as man's bodily death was to be once only. Such was the truth to be told to man. The words are these: "For CHRIST is not entered into the holy places made with hands, the figures of the true; but into heaven itself, now to appear in the presence of GOD for us: nor yet that HE should offer HIMSELF often, as the High Priest entereth into the holy place every year with blood of others; for then must HE often have suffered since the foundation of the world: but now *once* (απαξ, *once for all*) in the end of the world (completion of the ages) hath HE appeared to put away sin by the sacrifice of HIMSELF. And as it is appointed unto men once (*for all*) to die, but after this the judgment: so CHRIST was *once* (*for all*) offered to bear the sins of many," etc. (Heb. ix. 24—28.) Well may we ask, Were words ever plain and intelligible, if these words are not? Now we know that the doctrine gradually received into the Churches, was that CHRIST was to be *offered up again* as a sacrifice for sin. He was to be thus offered in the Communion, or what was afterwards called, "*The Mass.*" And HE was to be offered up as a new Sacrifice for sin, in a way entirely *new*, through the hands of earthly priests. And these new sacrifices for sin were to be as necessary for man's salvation as the great Sacrifice on Calvary. No contradiction can be imagined greater than this statement of *inspired* Scripture, and the uninspired statement made by the "Church" (so calling itself), in the course of a few centuries.

The error began in a superstitious view of the bread and wine after their consecration by the elders. In the *reserving* of the bread and wine thus consecrated, for such people who could not be present at the Church meeting, and in the extraordinary efficacy supposed to exist in the bread and wine, as conferring *immortality* on the bodies of believers. Ignatius (A.D. 101) says (Letter to Ephes. xx.), "Obeying your Bishop and the presbytery with an entire affection; breaking *one bread, which is the medicine of immortality, our antidote that we should not die,* but live for ever with the LORD."

Irenæus (A.D. 167) advances a still further step in this error of putting the outward bread and wine in the place of HIM whom they commemorate. In his work "Against Heresies," he says (book iv., ch. xxxiv., p. 327. Oxford, 1702), "In the *sacrifice* (*i.e.*, of the Eucharist) we show forth the communion and union of flesh and spirit; for as the food when the name of GOD is invoked over it, becomes *no longer common food*, but Eucharist; compounded of two things, the one earthly, the other heavenly; so, our bodies, receiving the Eucharist, *are no longer corruptible, but possessed of the hope of eternal life.*"

Tertullian speaks of "believers partaking of the grace of the Eucharist, by the cutting up and distributing of the LORD'S body, in the same manner as the flesh of a victim was distributed at a sacrifice." (Tertullian against Maran.)

Within my limited space, I cannot of course lead the reader through the gradual "development" (as it is now called) of this gross and material "Eucharist." Those who have not read, or cannot read the early "Fathers," from Clement to Tertullian (A.D. 192), will find a clear statement of the monstrous doctrine in Mr. Osburn's able book, called "Doctrinal Errors of the Apostolical and Early Fathers" (pp. 97—109).

No doubt the culmination of this extraordinary dogma was not fully reached till the Council of Trent made it to be "an Article of the faith," binding as essential upon the souls of men. The same doctrine is virtually held as to priest and sacrifice, by the Greek Church: "We therefore confess that the sacrifice of the Mass is one and the same with that of the cross; ... and the oblation of the cross is *daily renewed in the Eucharistic sacrifice.* ... The *priest*, invested with the character of CHRIST, changes the substance of the bread and wine into the substance of HIS real body and blood." ("Catechism of Council of Trent," p. 249 of Donovan's translation. 1829.)

Here, then, we see the subtle design of the great enemy of Truth. Not only was a new atoning sacrifice to be offered, but that sacrifice must be offered *through man's* intervention. *Without a human priest it could not be offered.* Man was thus made to be an intermediate *Saviour* of his fellow-men.

To what a pitch of majesty, then, and authority, was the priest to be lifted up! He at last became, according to the so-called Catholic doctrine, a superhuman being. Jewish priests had great dignity, but they only offered the blood of lambs, of goats, of bullocks. Christian *priests* were to take in their polluted hands the real body of the ETERNAL WORD, made flesh. The people, or laity, could only look with awe upon them. The *"brethren"* were divided by a gulf impassable from the *priest*. Hence the degraded state of any people who are placed under this priestly system. Men (the people) have practically no individual responsibility. Their very conscience is in the priest's hands. In religion they are mere passive children. Hence the state of France,

Italy, Spain, and Austria. Hence, too, the state of Ireland.

But what of priesthood in England? we may ask. Is there any such doctrine of priesthood amongst ourselves? One of the most unfortunate errors into which many of our English "Reformers" fell, was to retain the title of "priest" for the sacred order of pastors in the Church established by law. It is true that the mere name of "priest" would have done little harm to its bearers or to their Church, had it been explained to mean a simple *presbyter* or elder. And such is the meaning of "priest" which a large part of the clergy have always given to this word. "For," say they, "our Church gives us no real priestly functions, such as the old Catholic Church gave to its priests. *We* only offer sacrifices of prayer, praise, and the *commemoration* of the LORD's death in the Communion. Why not let us retain the name 'priest'?"

Our answer is obvious. If you have no real priestly functions, why be called priests? If the mere title, without its functions, be of no valid use or meaning to you, why so anxious to keep it? The fact is that Cranmer and his fellow-labourers *knew* quite well, when they drew up their first and second Prayer-books (in Edward the sixth's reign), that this title of *"priest" was never given to ministers during the Apostles' time.* They *knew* that for the space of 1,200 years the higher clergy had been called "priests," *because* they were believed to offer a new sin-atoning sacrifice. Cranmer *knew* that the Eastern and Western Churches used the term as interchangeable with that of elder. Our English "Reformers" *knew* that the foreign reformed Churches had rejected the title of *"priest,"* because they believed it to be unscriptural and dangerous. Why then retain the title?

It is not so clear that Cranmer intended to sweep away all unlawful priestly functions from the "reformed" clergy. English Church history proves that he did not act in these matters without serious warnings from his more consistent brethren in England, and from many who would have put away the *name* as well as the functions of the Romish priest. Cranmer and his friends, in drawing up their "Ordination" services, borrowed an important part of the Roman Ordinal. In giving the ministerial commission to the candidates, the latter are thus addressed by the Bishop: "Receive the HOLY GHOST for the *office and work of a priest* in the Church of GOD. . . . Whose sins thou dost forgive, they are forgiven; and whose sins thou dost retain, they are retained." (See Palmer's "Origines Liturgicæ," vol. ii., compared with "Pontificate Romanum," vol. ii.) It is remarkable that in the Romish Ordinal we find the title "presbyter" put for that of *"priest."* But in Cranmer's and (after him) Archbishop Parker's

Ordination Service, as well as in the Latin version of the Thirty-nine Articles, *sacerdos*, not *presbyter*, is the title given to the second order, *sacerdos* being the *Jewish* priest. (See Articles 32 and 36.) So also we read in a later work of Cranmer, called "The Power of the Keys," and in the Latin preface to the Ordination Service, " Bishops, priests, and deacons," are translated " *Episcopi, sacerdotes, diaconi.*"

By good men we are constantly told that the words, "Whose sins ye forgive," etc., convey no idea of power to forgive, such as the Romish priest claims. The words mean simply, "Declare and pronounce to His people, being penitent, the absolution and remission of their sins." You tell the penitent that "HE pardoneth and absolveth all them that truly repent," etc. Such is the just commission belonging to all true ministers of the Gospel, etc.

Much may be said on this ground. We doubt not the sincerity of those who thus argue, but we say that they have blinded themselves (by habit, as men so often do when favourite "traditions" are attacked) to *pervert the plain meaning of words.* Surely the danger of these unscriptural titles and commissions in the Prayer-book, has sufficiently proved itself during the last thirty-five years. Since that time, probably one-third of our clergy have learned to believe themselves *priests*, in the Jewish sacrificial sense of the term. Is it not high time to do away this

H

dangerous title, with the unscriptural formula of commissioning ministers which it now accompanies?

We are threatened with a "revision" of our incomparable English Bible. Is not a "revision" of the Prayer-book of far more pressing importance? Very little, if any false doctrine has been extracted from the erroneous translations of a word in HOLY SCRIPTURE. *Thousands* of men, on the other hand, believe themselves to be real priests, because a Bishop said to them, "Receive the HOLY GHOST for the office and work of a priest."

But the danger does not end in words which are interpreted so differently by different men. Cranmer, and after him Parker, set forth another formula of "absolution." In the "Visitation of the Sick" Office are contained the following *rubric* and declaration: "Here shall the sick person be moved to a special confession of his sins, if he feel his conscience troubled with any weighty matter; after which confession the *priest shall absolve him* (if he humbly and heartily desire it), after this sort: . . . By HIS authority committed to me, I ABSOLVE THEE FROM ALL THY SINS, in the name of," etc.

The words are no longer, "I declare and pronounce to you the forgiveness of sins," but "I absolve you." Authority is given to the priest to absolve us. Such teaching as this ought to be expunged from the Prayer-book. The best proof that this Visitation

Service is thought improper and inconsistent with the general standard of Scriptural teaching in the Prayer-book, is, that the far greater number of our best clergymen never offer to use it. They are, I believe, ashamed to see it in the book.

To answer that no independent nor inherent power of "absolving" is claimed for our "priests," but that they do so by authority of CHRIST," is merely to repeat what every Romish or Greek priest will tell you as to his DIVINE commission. It is "as GOD" that he absolves the penitent. We dispute and deny that DIVINE "authority" is given to Roman, Greek, or English "priests," to say to a dying man, "I absolve thee."

Why, then, we again ask, did Cranmer and Parker leave such dangerous words and such false ministerial assumptions in this Office? The answer is that Cranmer only emerged gradually from that Romanism in which he had been reared, that Papal system in which he had been ordained a Bishop; and that even after Edward the Sixth's accession, he *dared* not boldly to throw off all its "traditions." Secondly, Archbishop Parker, less of a bold Reformer than was Cranmer, dared not offend Queen Elizabeth by a thorough removal of Romish ritual.

Should any one be desirous to see these assertions *proved*, I refer him to a short comparison between the first and second Prayer-books of King Edward the

Sixth, as compared with that of Elizabeth, which I place in an appendix. The main reason for the retaining so much of Romish ritual, was doubtless the vain hope of *conciliating* the many Roman Catholic priests and people who for a time conformed to the "reformed" services, Liturgy, etc. Dr. Cardwell's learned book called "A History of the Prayer-book Conferences," will prove that Queen Elizabeth and her intimate advisers added those very significant words to the Communion Service which are uttered at the delivery of the bread and wine to the communicant. Words these, as Dr. Cardwell says, *"that might convey, though they would not necessarily involve the doctrine of the Real Presence."* So also did Elizabeth remove the important cautionary "declaration" respecting kneeling before the Communion Table, so wisely introduced by King Edward into his second book, and to the effect "that no adoration was done or ought to be done to any Real or Essential Presence." (See Cardwell's "Conferences," pp. 38—44.)

Of course, in proportion as Elizabeth's Prayer-book (which is virtually our present book) restored Romish rites or Romish terms attendant on the "Communion," in such proportion the notions of priestly power and office were "conveyed, though not necessarily involved," as Dr. Cardwell says, "concerning the Real Presence." Elizabeth next restored the "rubric of ornaments, vestments," etc., which Edward's second book had expunged. A great part of the Romish priestly Mass, vestments, and lighted candles, were thus by law enjoined on the clergy; and though a general disuse of these priestly dresses followed, as it were, by consent of clergy and people, the priestly rubric remains still a statute law, until Parliament and the Sovereign decree its removal. And I believe, that so long as these dangerous errors that prop up priestly assumptions remain parts of the Prayer-book, so long will thousands of clergymen deem themselves to be "Catholic *priests*," instead of Apostolic presbyters. So long will they go on nearer and nearer to the Roman apostacy, and so long will they mislead hundreds of deluded hearers to act more consistently than their deluded teachers : viz., to join Rome itself.

It may be urged that "All candidates for 'orders' who approach the solemn rite with earnest, believing prayer to GOD, will doubtless bring down upon their souls the SPIRIT's blessing, and new grace thereby to work in the ministry; so that it may be truly said, they in ordination 'receive the HOLY GHOST.'" New grace and life, no doubt, such believing prayer will call down upon their souls; but so will believing prayer on all other occasions bring down the same rich blessings. Still, spiritual "grace" and "life" are not the same as the "spiritual gifts" that we have been treating of in Part III. and IV. "Receive ye the HOLY GHOST:" when their LORD "breathed" these words on HIS Apostles, HE conveyed to them miraculous knowledge of HIS full Gospel truth, such as they had not before possessed. HE conveyed to them miraculous knowledge of the meaning of SCRIPTURE, and of its mysterious prophecies. "As yet they knew not the SCRIPTURE, that HE must rise from the dead." (John xx. 9.) Of the eleven Apostles it is said that "HE opened their understandings, that they should understand the SCRIPTURES." (Luke xxiv. 45.) The HOLY GHOST, who was "breathed" upon Apostles, was to "bring all things to their remembrance, whatsoever CHRIST had said unto them" (John xiv. 26): a gift surely miraculous. HE was "to show them things to come:" another miraculous gift. (John xvi. 13.) HE was to "lead them into all the truth" (John xvi. 13), so that they could declare and write down for our guidance "the whole counsel of GOD." (Acts xx. 27.)

Up to the time of the SPIRIT's descent, most of the Apostles were "ignorant and unlearned men." (Acts iv. 13.) As Galilean peasants, or fishermen, they knew not letters, "not having learned." (John vii. 16); much less could they read the Hebrew Bible; or the Greek version of it, the Septuagint; or the Pentateuch, written in the Samaritan dialect. If they were now made able to read the SCRIPTURE it must have been by *miracle.*

What we contend is, that by and at a Bishop's

"laying on of hands," not any spiritual gift, properly so-called, has been or is imparted, such as followed our DIVINE LORD's words, "Receive ye the HOLY GHOST." Most dangerous was it then for Cranmer and Parker to retain these words in their service. The service has puffed up too many ordained men with the notion that they had received what they never received. Hundreds who went into the Church, as it is called, in order to get a moderate income without much work, to belong to a genteel profession, or to take a "family living," have believed themselves DIVINELY called, and to be "successors of the Apostles." Many more thousands of people, shocked at such contradiction between reality and profession, leave the national Church for ever. How can this be wondered at in those who seek spiritual instruction for their souls? who cannot live upon the husks of outward ministerial titles and supposed Apostolic commissions without Apostolic grace or gifts?

No proof is there that any man of feeble intellect has left the Cathedral with an enlarged and vigorous understanding. No man deficient hitherto in critical knowledge of Scripture, has been suddenly filled with such knowledge; no man hitherto slow of utterance, hesitating and confused in his speaking, has been at once made to be clear and fluent in writing or speaking. The "gifts" of "teaching," "exhortation," "prophecy," or speaking in foreign tongues, have been never once miraculously given upon a Bishop's ordination. Enlarged and comprehensive knowledge of "all the truth" has never flashed upon those who before-time had not been even prayerful students of SCRIPTURE. In all these cases ordination has left a man where it found him. And men in general are too honest to avow that they have received any supernaturally sudden "gift."

What is most important to the ordained man, and to the people who are called his flock, no record have we that a man, heretofore worldly and unrenewed in heart, has, at his ordination, undergone that mighty change which our LORD has called "being born again," and which the SPIRIT has defined as a passage "from darkness unto light," and a rising "from death unto life." (Eph. v. 8; Rom. vi. 11.) Thus neither has the regenerating SPIRIT, nor miraculous "gifts of the SPIRIT," ever followed or accompanied (as far as evidence has reached us) any ordination by a Bishop, no more than by a Presbytery.

In an Appendix to this work, I put down some remarks upon the Defence which the present Bishop of Manchester has lately given to us of this Ordination Commission. This Defence may be taken as a fair specimen of the inconclusive reasoning with which many good and learned men are satisfied.

On the whole subject of revising the Liturgy, and of bringing the Ordination and other Services to a more Scriptural standard, I refer the reader to the following petition, which a large number of the Irish Church laity have signed and presented to their General Synod. We may cordially wish that in England laymen would do the same:—

From the "RECORD" *Newspaper of May 3rd,* 1872.

"Having seen that an address from certain members of the Irish Church, deprecating any revision of the Prayer-book, was presented to the General Synod by his Grace the Lord Primate, we, as members of the Irish Church, feel imperatively called upon to present a counter declaration, lest our silence should be misconstrued into indifference or hostility with reference to the great question of Liturgical Revision, in which we as Churchmen are deeply interested. We beg leave to state—

"I. That, considering the retrograde character of the alterations made in our Prayer-book, in the reigns of Elizabeth, James I., and Charles II., it is the bounden duty of all who regard the Reformation of the sixteenth century as the result of an outpouring of the Holy Spirit on the minds and hearts of our Reformers, to frustrate by a searching and thorough revision of our Prayer-book the persistent attempt to bring back our Church into bondage to 'the tyranny of the Bishop of Rome and all his detestable enormities,' from which, by God's blessing, we were delivered at the Reformation.

"II. That we regard with much satisfaction what has already been accomplished by the joint labours of the Revision Committee and the Synod. We allude particularly to the eliminating of the Apocrypha from the Lectionary, the removal of the names of the apocryphal saints from the calendar, and the rubric to be prefixed to the Morning Service, declaring that whenever the word 'priest' occurs, it is to be understood as meaning nothing more than presbyter; but we must express an earnest hope that the necessity of such a rubric will be obviated by the total removal of the word priest as designating any order of ministry.

"III. We are deeply persuaded that no revision will satisfy the requirements of Scriptural truth, and the desire of the earnest members of our Church, which does not include the following particulars:—

"1. The total ignoring of any judicial authority or power of our ministers in the matter of absolution. To accomplish this, the form of absolution in the service for the Visitation of the Sick should be totally expunged, and also the reference to this matter in the address to intending communicants, in our Communion Service. We must also get clean rid of the following sentences in the service for the Ordering of Priests:—'Receive the Holy Ghost for the office and work of a priest in the Church of God, now committed unto thee by the imposition of our hands. Whose sins thou dost forgive they are forgiven, and whose sins thou dost retain they are retained.' So long as such statements hold a place in the Prayerbook, it is vain to expect that any effectual check can be given to the anti-Christian sacerdotalism which has produced such calamitous results in England, and which is 'eating as doth a canker' in our Irish Church.

"2. The sentences which mar the perfection of the most solemn and impressive service for the Burial of the Dead, by imposing on the minister the necessity of using what is regarded as the language of assurance with reference to the salvation of the departed, should be omitted.

"3. The expressions in our Communion Service, and also in our Church Catechism, which seem to favour the notion of an objective presence of Christ in the Sacrament, must be removed. The following sentence in the Catechism, descriptive of the supposed 'inward and spiritual grace' of the Lord's Supper, is specially objectionable:—'The body and blood of Christ, which are verily and indeed taken and received by the faithful in the Lord's Supper.'

"4. The sentences in the Baptismal Service and the Catechism which seem to assert that every baptized infant is *ipso facto* 'regenerated,'—'born again,'—

'regenerated by the Holy Spirit,'—'made a member of Christ,'—'grafted unto His holy Church,'—constituted 'the child of God by adoption, and an inheritor of the kingdom of heaven.' These sentences, and every other expression which may be construed into an assertion of the effect of the Sacrament, should be totally expunged. Interpreted according to the plain meaning of the words as they now stand, they contain the essence of sacramentalism, and should have no place in the formularies of a Church reformed according to the model of Scripture. The use of the sign of the cross in baptism, and the appointment of godfathers and godmothers, are confessedly human ordinances, and their use or disuse should be left to the conscientious convictions of parents bringing their children to Christ's holy baptism. As the law of the Church now stands, no minister is authorized to baptize an infant, except on the condition of compliance with these unauthorized requirements. No Church has a right to impose such a condition.

"IV. We cannot conclude this declaration of our convictions with reference to the necessity of liturgical revision, and the particulars which are absolutely needful for such a measure of revision as we could accept, without expressing our determined adherence to the Irish Church. We love our Church for her faithful testimony to the essential truths of

Christianity contained in her Articles, and her equally faithful testimony against the manifold errors and superstitions wherewith the fallen Church of Rome has corrupted and obscured the Gospel of the grace of God. We approve of her episcopal government and threefold order of ministry, as justified by apostolic precedent. We accept her parochial arrangements as the best organization for effectual opposition to the hierarchy and priesthood of apostate Rome, and for the universal diffusion throughout the land of the knowledge of scriptural truth. We admire her admirable Liturgy, fervent without fanaticism, and sublime in its simplicity, expressing the deepest devotional feelings of a regenerated soul; and because we prize our Prayer-book, we are anxious to divest it of the incrustations of error, which, in the natural tendency of our fallen nature, have from time to time grown upon it, marring its beauty, and diminishing its efficiency.

"We regard the objectionable statements to which we have alluded in this declaration, and all of which have been foisted into our Prayer-book, or intensified in the three revisions to which it has been subjected since the time of Edward VI., as 'the dead flies, which cause the ointment of the apothecary to send forth a stinking savour.' Are we, therefore, because we abhor the conservatism of corruption which would retain these extraneous elements in our Liturgy, to be held up to odium as levelling revolutionists who would 'tear the Prayer-book to tatters'? In the consciousness of the injustice of such a charge we can patiently endure it, in the full persuasion that if our suggestions be carried out by the General Synod, the borders of our Church, by God's blessing, will be enlarged, and her efficiency promoted, to an extent which will make her such an instrument of good as she has never hitherto been in the midst of this land."

PART VII.

Present Means of Gospel Instruction in our Great Cities inadequate.

Need of Lay Preaching.

PART VII.

Present Means of Gospel Instruction in our Great Cities inadequate.

Need of Lay Preaching.

FROM what has been proved, it appears that preaching of the Gospel by unordained believers is lawful and necessary; and especially so when, at our very door, great masses of our fellow-men are lying in ignorance of a SAVIOUR. If forbidden and hindered from thus preaching by the pastors and rulers of Churches, lay-brethren must preach CHRIST in spite of all such opposition. They must obey GOD rather than man. If zealous brethren are thus called to preach, we believe that they should try to labour in concurrence with their pastors and their Church, and to ask their prayers. In this way, much enmity and needless divisions might often be avoided; and we should not see those isolated efforts that earnest brethren often carry on, and allow to drift into new Churches.

It is but a *truism* to say that the great populations of our large towns have no sufficient number of settled and ordained pastors to teach them the truth of God. And if there were settled pastors in ten-fold larger numbers than at present, it does not follow either that those pastors would in general be qualified to interest our rougher people, or that the people would place themselves under the present system of pastoral teaching.

"Evangelists," or preachers, are the class of men needed to go forth into our crowded streets. Such preachers must go *to* the people; they cannot wait for the people to go to them. The pastor's office and work pre-suppose a Church already gathered, amongst whom he ministers. The *evangelist* goes forth in order to gather souls into a Church; or rather, he goes to gather souls to the knowledge of a Saviour.

London naturally first strikes us, on account of its enormous population and their crying spiritual need. From the new census, as stated generally, more than three millions and a quarter of our fellow-creatures inhabit the vast area called London. That area includes all the Surrey side of the Thames river, together with a part of Essex and of Kent. I cannot anywhere get accurate returns of the number of clergymen, and of Trinitarian Nonconformists, who minister in churches and chapels throughout this

GOSPEL INSTRUCTION INADEQUATE. 115

mighty population; neither can I get accurate statistics of the number of people who generally attend churches or chapels. According to the "London Diocesan Year-book," the number of clergy who officiate within the Bishop of London's diocese, is only 1270. But I cannot ascertain what number of clergymen act in the Winchester diocese, nor of those who act under the Bishop of Rochester, within the Essex and Kent districts. Owing to the large area covered by the Surrey, Kent, and Essex sides of the Thames, we must suppose the clergy in those districts as numerous as the "London" clergy. We may reckon the whole number of clergymen at 2,500. We first deduct from the whole population 200,000 Roman Catholics (chiefly Irish); from the three millions thus left, we deduct one third for children up to the age of eleven years. Most of such children from six to eleven years are taught in Sunday-schools. Two millions then of adult and young people remain to call for religious instruction.

The number of Episcopal clergy, as I have said, may be put down at 2,500; the number of Trinitarian Nonconformist ministers I reckon to be about 500. I judge this from the "Year-books" of the Methodist, Baptist, and Congregational bodies. Whether Presbyterians, Primitive Methodists, and smaller Christian bodies, make up 100 more ministers, I cannot say: probably they do so. The total number of regular ministers will thus be 3,100. If we divide the two millions of people by 3,100 ministers, a congregation of 650 people might be taught by each minister. But we know that ministers and people cannot be thus equally assorted: and it does not follow that all these ministers are properly qualified to teach these people, even if the people could be brought to listen to their teaching.

Strictly speaking, we must reckon on a third part of the child population of London as included in the various congregations over which ministers preside. We must thus add more than 300,000 persons to the aggregate of supposed congregations.

Another general test by which to try the number of people in London who hear religious teaching, is by ascertaining the number of sittings which churches and chapels contain, and the average number of people who occupy them on Sundays. But here we can get no accurate information. We know that many of the larger churches hold from 1,500 to 2,000 sitters; many small chapels hold only from 300 to 400. If we reckon the whole number of churches and chapels to be 1,000 (a large estimate), and if we reckon that on an average 600 people attend each of these churches and chapels on Sundays, there would be 600,000 people so attending. But does any common observer believe that this large number do regularly fill these sanctuaries of London? Let such observer

GOSPEL INSTRUCTION INADEQUATE. 117

walk along the "New Cut," in Southwark, on a Sunday morning, at eleven a.m.; or let him at that same hour look at the masses of people that stream along Whitechapel Road. In the "New Cut" there is a crowded market. In either case let the observer see the hives of men and women there swarming,— buying, selling, lounging: he will see enough to convince him that a great part of London people neglect all religious ordinances; that they attend neither chapel nor church. In other words, if out of the three million adults and children, *one million* of them both attend some religious teaching occasionally or constantly; and if we put aside from this number 500,000 as infants, aged and sick people; how are the *million and a half* yet to be accounted for? This million and a half have practically nothing to do with churches, chapels, or their ministers, except in the matters of baptism, marriage, and burial.

Then of what order is the average teaching given by these 2,400 ministers, as far as it regards the little educated classes and the poor? Are not a large part of the "*sermons,*" read or repeated, clothed in words and with phrases which our poorer brethren cannot understand? If so, "he that speaketh," speaketh almost in a " tongue *unknown* " to his hearers. Then in the larger *parish* churches or chapels, *where* are the poorer brethren placed? Generally in the sittings most distant from the minister, and where hearing is the most difficult. St. James's description is generally verified. We say "to the brother of low degree, Sit thou yonder!" while *I* (the richer, "with the gold ring," the well-dressed, and the more educated) say, "I sit *here!*" Sometimes indeed the poorer brethren are billeted on the public gaze, *as poor*, in certain short cramped benches, which fill up part of the middle interval between the pews of the rich. Could we persuade, could we even ask our poorer brethren, now loitering the Sabbath away, to go into such "*free* seats"? Could we honesty say to the bystanders in the "New Cut," or in Whitechapel, "You ought, my friends, to be in a church or chapel this morning"? "Pray, sir, tell us in what church or chapel one fiftieth part of us could find room?" Or would not some shrewd listener to our Pharisaic question reply, "Go and preach to your rich people, who attend these churches and chapels, to build plain rooms for us, and send plain speakers to teach us the plain truths of the Gospel. We shall then believe that you are in real earnest about our souls."

And what could we answer to this just reply, but that the mass of our rich and great men do attend their churches and chapels, but that they are mostly "religious *to themselves*." They have given large sums, it may be, to build ornamental churches; but they have left no money for building plain rooms, in which plain evangelists could speak the Gospel.

But London has other means of giving Gospel instruction to the people, it may be said, than what 1,000 churches and chapels can give. We have about 330 missionary teachers sent out by the "London City Mission." These are all good, earnest men. They are chosen on account of their piety, and their general fitness for visiting and speaking to our workmen population. These missionaries belong to different Protestant (Trinitarian) Churches. There is also a "Church of England *Scripture Reader's* Society," the number of whose "readers" I am not now able to ascertain. It is not, however, large. The Church of England "*Lay Helpers*' Association" appears also to send out a good many godly, earnest men, for the purpose of visiting and reading Scripture to many of the poorer brethren whom the clergyman cannot reach. We cannot suppose that less than 500 city missionaries and "readers" visit through a large part of London. If we reckon four persons as an average family, and three or four hundred families as being visited and instructed by every missionary or reader, we have an aggregate of 1,200,000 adult persons instructed more or less in the truths of religion; at least, some offer of teaching is made to them; and the destitution of religious teaching is thus not so crying as at first sight it seemed to be.

Again: we must not forget that from eighty to one hundred zealous men, under the "Open-air Mission," preach through many parts of London during the fine weather; and that thus tens of thousands hear of a SAVIOUR's message, who probably would never hear it within church or chapel, nor even listen to the missionary when he visited their houses. I believe such evangelism to be, under all our present circumstances, the most likely to reach the hearts of what we must call "irreligious street-hearers." Then we have preaching in several London theatres during part of the year. Ordained ministers and unordained "evangelists" have lifted up a SAVIOUR's cross to multitudes within those walls. Sometimes from ten to fifteen thousand people have thus been got together on a Sunday evening. The listeners who have attended these services have been, to a large extent, drawn from that class which goes neither to church nor chapel. But they have listened reverently; and, we trust, in numerous cases "believed, to the saving of the soul."

We may next take Manchester, our second city, as a second illustration of our subject. According to the census of 1871, the whole population of Manchester and its neighbour townships must be 800,000 souls. As in the case of London, from these 800,000 we at once deduct for infants and children up to a certain age, *one third;* or, in round numbers, 270,000 persons. For Roman Catholics and others who would not receive religious instruction from our evangelists, we may, I believe, deduct one fifth,—that is to say, 160,000 more: to this add 270,000: total deducted, 430,000. Add to these 77,000 provided for in Church of England churches, and 40,000 more accommodated in Nonconformist chapels, we deduct 117,000 more from the gross total. That is to say, we have a residue of 303,000 souls of adult men and women who do not attend church or chapel, and for whose attendance, did they wish it, no sittings could be at present provided. From the "Diocesan Year-book" of 1871, I find that there are seventy-seven churches and licensed rooms under the Established Church; and that about 77,000 sittings are provided in these buildings. From the four large Nonconformist Church returns, I find about 40,000 sittings provided by Methodist, Baptist, Independent, and Presbyterian chapels. The total sittings therefore, *if occupied* by sitters, would make out 117,000 attendants. We know however, practically, that in very few churches or chapels are all seats ever filled.

In Manchester, too, as well as in London, we have our fair proportion of "city missionaries," "Scripture readers," and "district visitors." The two latter classes are generally sent out by some distinct religious communion. We have above ninety city missionaries. Their whole time is given to the instruction of the thousands who generally neglect the outward ordinances of religion. If on the average each missionary visits 300 families of four persons each, 1,200 persons are thus visited by each missionary; or, in the aggregate, there will be, in round numbers, about 110,000 persons thus visited and instructed: and if fifty Scripture readers and visitors, employed by clergymen, Nonconformist ministers, and "laymen," be added to the missionaries, 60,000 more persons may receive, if they choose, some religious teaching. Out of the 303,000, therefore, whom we reckon as non-attendants at church or chapel, 80,000 or 90,000 may be deducted as occasional hearers of the "Word of Life." The number of people thus left *without any systematic teaching* may be reduced from 303,000 to 295,000 souls. But what a vast number is this of immortal creatures left almost unevangelized in one city! Upon the labours of our brethren in the London and Manchester "City Missions," I write with great confidence: I believe that the DIVINE blessing has come down, and is coming down, upon them most richly. For their piety, their clear view of Gospel truth, their kind manners, and their good sense, the missionaries are chosen by discerning Christian men. They are also truly *voluntary* workers; for though they receive a moderate payment for their service, it is but small compared with that which a different employment might bring them, had they chosen one. The special advantage which such missionaries have over all parochial clergymen or Nonconformist ministers, is that they give *time* sufficient for talking to each person whom they visit, time to explain Scripture to them (if asked), time to show sympathy with them in their sorrows, and time to deal with each case or character which comes before them. Still, with all these means of religious instruction in London and Manchester, and we may add, all our great manufacturing towns, we return to the great fact before us. A million and a half in London, and 300,000 in Manchester, are practically living in spiritual ignorance; such spiritual ignorance, that their outward habits, conduct, and appearance, bespeak either gross indifference to DIVINE truth, or opposition to it. Look at the surging mass of people who on Sunday crowd along Demsgate, in Manchester, just as the London people crowd Whitechapel Road, and you need no further proofs of what I say.

What then is to be done? I return to the point from which I set out at the beginning of this treatise. "Evangelists"—lay evangelists—must go forth in numbers to preach the news of saving mercy to these now unevangelized masses. I say lay preachers, because (1) all earnest ordained pastors have little or no time to leave their stated duties in their Churches; (2) because in the present state of disordered feeling which reigns amongst these city masses, those preachers are more likely to be listened to with respect who are *known* to labour for their souls' good *unpaid, and as having no official titles*—being neither "parsons nor priests"—names which these people generally give to regular ministers of the Word. We may, I know, lament or condemn such views and such words as these, so commonly used by our city masses. Nevertheless, the fact remains. Ministers are deemed to be *paid* professional men. *Unpaid* preachers, whether gentlemen, shopkeepers, or artizans, who are known to have no motive but the doing of good, these people are more predisposed to hear. And did not the great Apostle bow to such prejudices, when he told even professed believers, at Thessalonica, that himself, Silas, and Timotheus, "freely preached to them the Gospel of GOD," and "would not be chargeable" to them as the Apostles of CHRIST (1 Thes. ii. 9); or when he learned the humble art of "tentmaking," and wrought with his own hands for his daily bread, rather than ask a small pittance from the Church. (Acts xviii. 3.)

"Are we" tempted sometimes to say, "A certain amount of DIVINE truth is within the reach of the millions in London, and the hundreds of thousands in Manchester? What with the indoor and outdoor preachings, all these people might hear some truth, however little. That truth is near at their doors.

And if these masses will not avail themselves of any of these teachings, indoors or outdoors, the guilt lies with themselves. *We* have done our best; we are not answerable for doing more," etc.

Our consciences ought to give a speedy answer to such cold idleness: "Love thy neighbour as thyself." Where and what should WE now be had we been left to gather our religion from one or more stray addresses, given forth by an out-door preacher at the corner of a London street? Where should we be if our parents had set us no example of prayer, Scripture reading, and attendance on some religious teaching? Had we been taught that morals consisted in keeping out of prison, and as much of *good conduct* as would help us on in the world, do we believe that a few chance preachings would have led us to heartfelt, genuine conversion from sin to GOD? It might have been so. Such conversions have been; but such cases are almost miracles!

The best way of judging the process of man's conversion to GOD, is to look back on our own past lives. We perhaps had the unspeakable blessing of a pious, praying mother: we had then "precept on precept" in our childhood from the tenderest lips. *We* perhaps had religious teaching at a school: *we* perhaps were taken to hear the true Gospel preached by some holy minister. All these privileges were perhaps little valued by us at the time. The heart was little affected. It was not perhaps till manhood and the world's trouble came upon us, that the words of a praying mother, and of a faithful minister, returned with overwhelming power to us. Then we felt that we had not had *too much* of religious teaching.

And why should we judge differently for our poorer brother? Are we to be satisfied that he should hear a chance outdoor address now and then? Does he not need some regular teaching as well as ourselves? Shall we not try to supply his soul with more of that bread which has nourished our own, perhaps from childhood?

I grant this difference between rich and poor: viz., that the richer classes seem to need a ten-fold religious teaching to that which those need who work for daily bread. The richer are, upon inspired authority, more apt to have their "hearts over-charged with surfeiting and drunkenness and cares of this life" (Luke xxi. 34); "the cares of this world, and the deceitfulness of riches, and the lusts of other things" (Mark iv. 19): so that to the rich man, however correct be his outward religion and his inner doctrine, his entrance to heaven must ever be as the camel's—prostrate, ere he can pass through the "needle's eye" of humiliation and self-denial. It is "easier for a camel" to pass that low portal, than for "the rich man," etc.

To close this subject of outdoor preaching, recollect how small a number out of the London million and half gather to listen to an outdoor preacher. If fifty evangelists were to preach on a given Sunday, in London, *outdoors*, they would form one preacher for every 30,000 souls! We know that 500 persons are a large congregation to listen to any outdoor preacher. That is to say, if fifty preachers could all address 500 people at the same time, there would only be 25,000 persons preached to out of 1,500,000 : one sixth part of the whole unevangelized mass. What then, in sight of these masses of men almost neglected, can we or ought we to do ?

(1) Christian men of wealth and influence ought to build plain rooms, in which the Gospel might be taught simply and earnestly to the poor. At present their general practice is to spend large sums in building handsome churches and chapels. All this money so willingly given towards outward grandeur and beauty, suits in general the rich and the educated. We complain that so much money is spent for the rich, so little for the poor. We want the money not for grand buildings, but in order to pay zealous ministers who will teach our people the Gospel truth. I regard then as squandered on ornament the large sum of money which has been spent on towers, spires, and mediæval architecture; whilst scarcely any money has been given to endow zealous ministers who might preach to the poor in plain buildings or out of doors. The late Rev. HUGH STOWELL (of Salford), during

the year before his departure, told me what *he* desired for the good of the masses who inhabited his district, and who could not be visited, nor be accommodated within a church. It was the building of a plain school-room; the sittings free, or nearly so; and the proper payment of a zealous minister, who might attract many of the neglected people by real, heartfelt, plain speaking. Such was the "*memorial* church" he said he desired to be built after his decease. Should the poor gather round their teacher, and he not rapidly leave his flock, a church on a larger scale might come afterwards. Mr. S.'s wishes were not carried out; and the elegant church, which exhausted most of the subscription money, contains no larger proportion of the poor than attend other elegant churches; that is to say, a very small proportion. *We want plain buildings, free sittings, living, earnest preaching, and short services.* Will the rich merchants and land-owners come forward thus to provide the Gospel for the poor?

(2) We want our earnest clergymen and Nonconformist ministers to *encourage* godly laymen from amongst their flocks *to go forth as evangelists.* Instead of keeping up a paltry fear lest the lay preacher should be popular, let them simply weigh the actual state of the thousands near them, and their own hopeless inability to minister to their souls. If ministers would thus try to draw out the "gifts" of

godly laymen, they would bind many hearts nearer to themselves, which otherwise may be distanced and separated from themselves by cold neglect. Ministers may be assured that no great number of laymen will apply for their sanction in outdoor preaching. Certainly no mere worldly desire of praise and admiration will lead men to lift up their voices in a London or Manchester thoroughfare, in order to speak of things the most sacred, amidst sounds and sights the most uncongenial and disgusting, amidst the clatter of wheels, and often in sight of the gin-palace and its reeling company. Each earnest minister should gather around him and *instruct* a "school of prophets" for his district,—some for indoor meetings, and some for the streets. Many earnest lay preachers, ready to brave all difficulties and hindrances, are yet young believers. Their views of DIVINE truth, however glowing and bright, are often one-sided and ill-balanced; their statements are often crude. The counsel and sympathy of that minister who had led them to living truth, might be of the greatest use to such evangelists as these. They would also go forth to preach, followed by the prayers of the Church to which they belonged. Some brethren of that Church would go with them. Still their one object would be not to preach their Church as the best or only one: "The LORD JESUS CHRIST" is their ALL IN ALL!

On the other hand, we feel that zealous laymen,

who have both time to spare and gifts for such ministry,—such good men should pay some deference to the ministers of that Church with which they are in communion. Before such good laymen go forth thus to evangelize, they should consult, if possible, their minister's feelings. They should ask his consent and sanction of the object which they have in view: viz., *the wish not to establish a new Church or sect*, but simply to speak of a SAVIOUR to those who are sunk in irreligion.

Too many earnest evangelists, while repudiating the making of a sect, have fallen into a sect insensibly. This has generally followed the celebration of the Holy Communion by such evangelists. Though I can attach no holiness to that DIVINE rite, because of the ministers who preside over it (whether Episcopal or Presbyterian); yet I believe that godly ministers are appointed to hold the keys of Church discipline, and that their high office justly entitles them to *preside* over that which is most solemn in Church-worship,—not to say that many young and zealous evangelists are often led to consider high *professions* of conversion and much *emotional* religion as superior to that which is more quiet, but in reality more deep, in the view of those brethren who are more cautious and more instructed than themselves.

We have vindicated, I believe truly, the right and duty of laymen or brethren to teach and preach the

Gospel. We would also vindicate the right of godly pastors to that deference and respect which their constant "labouring in the Word and doctrine" deserves from preaching brethren. A layman, however zealous he be to bless the ignorant, will yet be modest and considerate towards the pastor who is as zealous as himself to do good, but who cannot so easily leave his beaten track to evangelize. Under our present distorted system of Church office-bearers and Church work, faithful pastors, who minister in large town districts, have burdens laid upon them which they cannot long bear. Where lay evangelists belong to the same communion in which these pastors labour so hard, evangelists should offer their services as a "help," and not as in apparent disregard of, and opposition to, their pastors.

"I beseech you, brethren, to know them which labour among you, and are over you in the LORD, and admonish you; and to esteem them very highly in love for their work's sake." (1 Thess. v. 12, 13.)

"Remember them who have the rule over you, who have spoken unto you the Word of GOD." (Heb. xii. 7.)

"Let all your doings be done with charity." (1 Cor. xvi. 14.)

PART VIII.

Appeal to the Gentry.

PART VIII.

Appeal to the Gentry.

IN looking at those myriads of our fellow-men, as they surge along Whitechapel or Deansgate, what earnest believer in GOD's truth but longs to stop and preach CHRIST unto them? Who wishes not that he had a voice to reach them, and a spiritual power to arrest their attention? At the moment we gaze upon them, we know that all the ministers of London and Manchester cannot reach them, and that most of the men whom we see seldom hear the missionary's or visitor's voices, because they are absent from their homes when the missionary calls.

This desire on our part is but the *common-sense* of religion within us. It is but the faint reflection of our SAVIOUR's mind: "When He saw the multitudes HE was moved with compassion, because they fainted, and were scattered abroad as sheep having no shepherd." (Matt. ix. 36.)

What then? We want hundreds, thousands of lay, of unordained preachers, to do what the ordained cannot do. We want them out of all classes of men. We want godly workmen, we want tradesmen, we want *gentlemen;* but we especially want the latter class—the educated and refined *gentleman.* And why? We want him for the purpose of a double sermon. The rich brother has not only to preach to the people because he loves their souls, he has also to preach *the practice* of that Gospel he would enforce. He has to show that the rich brother can take some trouble, can give part of his leisure time, can "go about doing good." It is to higher *practice,* showed forth by those called "religious people" amongst the rich and the refined, that our shrewd brethren of the factory look for. "If these rich religious people pity us so deeply, and speak of us at public meetings 'as so degraded and irreligious,' why do they not come forth to warn and instruct us?"

Blessed be God, that He has graciously enabled some of our nobles and gentry to take part in preaching the gospel to these masses of men. Still their number is at present so small, as to prove them *the exception* amidst their class.

Both in London and Manchester we find that the far greater number of out-door preachers to the street population is from the apprentices, the tradesmen, and the clerks. After their week's full labour they give that Sabbath, which they might spend in partial rest, to the calling of their fellow-men to repentance and to heaven. What then keeps back our godly rich men from doing the same? What good to souls might not fifty rich Christian men out of one hundred thus accomplish! We must all feel, upon reflection, that it is not so much the truth alone preached which goes to the hearer's heart. It is the preacher's own character, his life, his known *motives* for doing good.

Before I make a short final appeal to our "higher classes" upon this subject, I will place before the reader an extract from the *Times* newspaper, which will, I believe, commend itself to his judgment. It is dated October 13th, in 1871. A leading article appeared that day upon the Church Congress, then holding its sittings at Nottingham. Much was said at that Congress about the drunkenness, the general depravity, &c., of our great city populations: How were such evils to be met, was the problem. The *Times* first states that,—

"The masses of our people are not worse than when Galilæan fishermen went forth to evangelize them. There is a remedy which does, in a great measure, meet the difficulty, and which is ready to hand, if Church Congresses and Diocesan Synods and Conferences are really willing to put out their hand to take it,—*if they are prepared, in short, to do anything but talk.* A good deal has been said lately about the use of *Laymen. Lay* assistants, *lay* readers, *lay* almoners, and now, at last, of lay PREACHERS ... Of course this really comes to a new order of ministers; free to exercise secular callings, and incapable of what is called 'the cure of souls;' not tied to residence, and generally enjoying more liberty than it is expedient to allow to those who undertake the 'cure of souls.' No one can doubt that in many parishes, particularly in town parishes, there are many laymen well qualified, in all respects to assist the clergyman in his work .... How is the work to be done? How are the persons to do it? Almost everywhere are to be found gentlemen, and others of at least an educated class, who are good Christians, who are scholars, probably better scholars than their own clergy; who can read well, and speak well, and whose lives are a sufficient testimony to their disinterested zeal. *Nobody with the Apostolic Epistles in his hands can say that these persons may not teach, preach, and pray in public, even if they are still laymen in the ordinary sense of that word*. Take a parish of 20,000 souls, with the Incumbent always engaged .... and the Curate .... *are we to wait* .... when there are half a dozen laymen qualified to take their part in the Spiritual duties of a parish? Of course they would have to be recognised. It would be necessary, and they would wish it themselves. If such a suggestion .... seems to infringe on a *sacred monopoly*, we can only say that without some such plan, *the work will never be done*," &c.

I commend these common-sense conclusions from "the Apostolic Epistles" to many readers. It will not be thought that the *Times* advocates fanatical "ranting" or "sensational excitement" in preaching. The *Times* advocates a plain Scriptural duty—the duty which these pages have been written to prove and to enforce.

Concluding Appeal to the Christian Gentry.

LET us ask ourselves the simple, but truly solemn question: "When we die what soul on earth will be left behind us the better for our preaching or example? Or, to go further,—could we hope to meet one soul in heaven who could welcome us with those transporting words, 'Thou wast as an angel of GOD upon that dark sea below, to guide me to a SAVIOUR and to glory.'" I cannot but ask the question of others and of myself, What might not the Christian *Gentry*, scattered through the various Churches, do for the good of souls, did we employ those "gifts" with which we have been entrusted, in the best way? It must be owned that, as a class, we hold out but a feeble light, and hold but a low position. Our means of obtaining DIVINE knowledge, and of spreading that knowledge, are almost unexampled. From Sabbath to Sabbath most of us listen to a

Gospel that our minister teaches faithfully. Some of us hear it from ministers who enforce that Gospel with commanding power of argument and persuasion. We would not lose a sermon. But as we go home from our Chapel or Church does not the question knock at our hearts' door, "What are we doing for the ignorant neighbours who live near us?" Perhaps we attend some Church-service in London, in Liverpool, or in Manchester. Our path homewards may take us through some of those back streets and courts where the neglected neighbours live. Everything looks begrimed and sad as we hurry through them. Women sitting idle on their door-steps; men smoking and reading newspapers; lads, above the school age, playing upon patches of ground still unbuilt upon. Do we go to our quiet home, with all its charm and luxury,—to our comfortable dinners and pleasant gardens,—and do we resolve to do *nothing* on that sacred day for our poor neighbours' souls? Or can we really look upon their sad state, and coolly say, "Poor degraded beings!" And, Why does not the clergyman or his curate get amongst them? If they have no time, why not the city missionary, towards whose salary we give our yearly subscription? Why not the Scripture-reader, whom we also help to maintain?" &c. Can we *honestly* thus speak?

If we thus speak of clergymen who, as we know,

in large towns have the nominal charge of ten to 13,000 people, we know that they are already exhausted by labour. Like the Pharisees then of old, "we bind burdens" on the clergy "too heavy to be borne;" yet we ourselves touch "them not with one of our fingers." Oh, let us not think that clergymen, missionaries, Scripture-readers, are to act for us in all labours of love; and that if we pay them our money subscriptions, we are not answerable for any personal service. In the Apostles' Letters to the Churches, there is no such exemption from visiting and teaching our poorer brethren, *because we happen to be of what is called "an Upper Class" of human beings.*" One law of brotherly love streamed forth upon rich and poor from the Passover-room of Jerusalem. "If I, your LORD and Master, have washed your feet, ye ought also to wash one another's feet. For I have given you an example, that ye should DO AS I have done unto you." (John xiii. 14.) Perhaps the only thing which may stir the hearts of some degraded brethren living in those crowded streets, is the going amongst them by the rich merchant, whose money accumulates through those workmen's toil; or by the rich landowner, whose "fortune" and that of his children grows to a giant rental through the covering of his building-land by new streets and a thickened population. "The brother of low degree" may then begin to see that rich Christians are not too selfish to sit and talk with him about his earthly sorrows and his *eternal* welfare. Our poorer brethren do not measure our love to them by the subscriptions that we pay to city missionaries or to hospitals; such gifts on our part cost us no personal trouble or sacrifice. Our poor do not read printed reports, nor look to see if our names figure high or low upon the list of donors. But when we sit down and converse with him in his own house, or when we visit the sick child or wife upstairs, many a stern factory workman or rugged collier may begin to think that there is reality in the Gospel, because it brings down man's lofty looks, and can lead the self-indulgent seeker of money or pleasure, to give not only money which costs him nothing, not merely a little time spent at a charity committee, but somewhat of his heart and sympathy, with those fellow-men who have not had our vast advantages of religious teaching and family purity, but who have lived from their childhood amidst scenes of drunkenness, profanity, and profligacy.

"Wash one another's feet." By the "washing of a brother's feet," we understand the effort to rid a fallen fellow-man of some loathsome corruption: such would be a pleading with the drunkard by kind warning in friendly conversation. It may cost us some repulsive effort to sit with one whose dwelling and whose children are squalid through his unclean habits; but who can say how kind words from such a quarter would speak to the heart?

Is it, then, that men are *too rich*, *too noble* in title, either to visit the fatherless and widow, or to visit and teach our poorer brethren? Why so put off our Christian duty? *Too rich, too noble!* Do we say (as I have often heard it said), "It is better for paid visitors, whose rank in life brings them nearer to the poor, to visit the poor: if *I* go into a cottage, the poor woman's eye is turned directly to my money, and 'how much shall I get from him'?" Do we say, "The paid visitor is not so easily deceived by false stories of distress as *I* am. The visitor understands the habits and circumstances of the poor: he will inquire as *I* cannot do. He will then report to me who are proper objects for money relief: I shall then look to such applicants," &c., &c.

There is force in these statements, but they cannot obviate nor override the solemn words of GOD. The great day of account draws on. As *individuals* we shall be judged (Rom. xiv. 10—12),—not by what others did of good on our behalf, but for what we ourselves have done of good. "I was sick, and ye visited me: I was in prison, and ye came unto me." (Matt. xxv. 36.) The word is not, "You visited ME through others: you were too rich, too noble to go yourselves into a prisoner's dungeon, or a poor man's bed-room." Such reasons against our "coming down," find no favour *here*. The word is, "Let the rich (brother) rejoice in that he is *made low*." (James i. 9.) "Exhort them (the believers) who are rich in this world, that they be not high-minded . . . that they do good, that they be *rich in good works*, ready to distribute, willing to communicate," &c. (1 Tim. vi. 17—19.) And what "good works" can the rich brother do "to poorer brethren" more good than the doing of good to THEIR SOULS? We should be rich in such good works, "willing to distribute" the bread of life, and "ready to communicate" of the blessings unspeakable that we ourselves enjoy, of sin forgiven and a hope full of immortality.

It is quite possible that many godly "rich and titled" believers honestly think that by visiting and speaking of DIVINE truth to poorer brethren, they may encourage a religious profession which is hollow and mercenary. But it is equally important for the rich man to learn his own *real* motives for neglecting a plain duty. Are we not a little afraid of appearing niggardly towards poor men, when it is known how much we spend upon our houses, our gardens, our luxuries?

Of course we know that many a godly brother or sister of the "higher ranks" is justly disabled from thus visiting and teaching the poorer: they may be themselves infirm and sick; they may live at too great a distance. Their hearts travel in sympathy to the afflicted, where their feet cannot walk: "It was well that it was in thine heart." By HIM who "judgeth righteously" we know that their loving hearts will be commended: "She hath done what she could." But it is surely otherwise with those rich Christians whose mental and bodily strength enables them to attend their bank, or mercantile office, or brewery, during the six week days, and thus constantly to increase their store. Surely two hours of the LORD's Day, afternoon or evening, they might leave their palaces in some grand London square, in order to visit some court or lane not far distant, where hundreds pine in ignorance. Surely they could give up their pew-sittings at the evening Sunday-service, for the use of some who need instruction. Religious "services," even the most spiritual preachings, are but means to attain a great end: *viz.*, our growth in holy action, as well as in holy knowledge or holy desires. What good in repeated "Sermons" and Liturgies which do not help to drive us out of our false ease and indolence?

But what may we say of the gentry and nobles who have no hard weekly work to do in what we call "business," or what we call a "profession"? (I speak of those who have received the Gospel into their hearts: I trust there are many thousands such). When such good men live in London "for the season," what spiritual good do they attempt for the unevangelized? Do they go only to mingle in the society of their equals, or go to minister to those below themselves? Do they go to enjoy what are called "the reasonable pleasures" of London, and leave nothing behind of real good to souls? I confess that what, thirty years ago, I saw of what is called "*high*" religious society," gave me the most dreary view of its inability to further vital religion in my own heart or in that of others. And when after the groaning dinner, and evening *party*, we were asked to join in the hymn of "Pilgrims and strangers, travelling through this *wilderness*," I felt afraid of travelling through a land of gilded Phariseeism, and of speaking against *worldliness* whilst I was clothed in its most refined form. Conscience whispered that we were trying to make the most of *both worlds*. It was an escape to leave the place.

When these gentry and nobles return to their country mansions, I trust it may be to work actively for the spiritual good of the poor around them. But I believe I do not exaggerate when I say that but very few of them go forth to teach or preach the Gospel. Many of our gentry can speak fluently at political meetings or on county business. Would that they spoke life-giving words of eternal truth in the cottage, or in the school-room, or in the field!

As to *Lay Preaching*, rich brethren, no more than

poor brethren, can be all "preachers" in the wider sense of that term. But if so, cannot rich brethren pay an additional missionary who can preach the glad tidings? Cannot rich believers who belong to the Church of England, pay an additional curate to help their minister, and to preach the simple truth in school-rooms or out of doors? Cannot all wealthy brethren do far more than they now do, to spread their SAVIOUR's kingdom upon earth?

Oh, could we stir up rich and educated believers thus to act amidst our large town populations, might we not hope that thousands would see the transporting vision of GOD in CHRIST? Might we not hope that "rivers would break forth in the desert, and streams in the dry places!"

Let us make the trial. Let us leave the gilded drawing-room and the easy arm-chair. Let us leave the insipid talk of the lips *about* religion, which "tendeth only to poverty," and ends in no vigorous *work*. Let us pray that we may leave the city, or town, something better than we found it.

APPENDIX.

(I.) TO PART VI.

On the motives which led Queen Elizabeth to reject some of the Improvements which the second Prayer-book of Edward VI. contained, and to prefer his first Book.

(See Cardwell's "Conferences," p. 34—36.)

"FROM this comparison, then, of the two Books of Common Prayer, it appears to have been the persuasion of the Queen and her Council, that in the important questions of the Eucharist and clerical vestments, *too much had been done in the reign of King Edward, in the way of innovation;* that the mysteries of religion had been impugned by excluding words that might suggest, though they would not necessarily involve the doctrine of the REAL PRESENCE; and the authority of the Church had been injured in the alteration respecting vestments. On the first point, accordingly, the words addressed individually to the communicant were now made to combine the two separate forms of the time of King Edward. With the same view also was expunged the rubric, which had been added to the Communion Service by that King on his own authority, after the publication of his second Liturgy; declaring '*that no adoration was done, or ought to be done, to any Real or Essential Presence there being of* CHRIST's *natural flesh and blood.*' To these changes no reasonable objection could be made (*i.e.*, by Roman Catholics or Anglicans) on either side. The Romanists could not disapprove of what they held to be improvements," etc., etc., etc.

Thus, as far as Elizabeth was concerned, she would have allowed no warning against *adoring the Sacramental emblems*, as if CHRIST were present in them. Edward's second book had said, "As concerning the Sacramental bread and wine, they remain still in their very natural substances, and therefore may not be adored; for that were *idolatry*, to be abhorred of all faithful Christians." This "declaration" about kneeling, and against idolatry, was restored to the Communion Service as it now stands at the last review of the Prayer-book, in 1661. (See Cardwell's "Conferences;" and Dr. Blackeney's elaborate "History of the Prayer-book," second edition, p. 413.)

Elizabeth's, and her Council's, motives in thus going backwards are obvious. She preferred more of ritual and ceremonial in religious services than the more consistent Reformers had set up, or which Edward's second Prayer-book had retained. To the last, Elizabeth had candles lighted upon the Communion Table in her private chapel. She also persevered in objecting to the marriage of clergymen; next, the Queen's, and her advisers', motive was, that by a designed ambiguity of language in the Communion Service, Roman Catholics might, after all, believe that that service admitted the "Real Presence." Could any thing but failure and confusion follow such a compromise with dangerous error?

II.

The Term "Priest."

IF we examine our present Prayer-book (which is substantially that of Queen Elizabeth), we shall find the name "Priest" to be very often used in the Sacramental Services of Baptism and the "Communion." The "priest" is made to do the acts that are most significant in these ordinances : *e.g.*, "The *priest* standing at the north side of the LORD's Table."

"Then shall the *priest*, turning *to* the people, still kneeling," etc.

"The *priest* shall read the Gospel."

"The *priest* shall return to the LORD's Table."

"The *priest* shall place upon the Table so much bread and wine," etc.

"After which the *priest* shall say," etc.

"The communicants being conveniently placed, the *priest* shall say."

"Then shall the *priest* say to them that come to receive," etc.

"Then shall the *priest* (or Bishop), turning himself to the people, *pronounce the absolution*."

"Then shall the *priest* say."

"After which the *priest* shall proceed," etc.

"Then shall the *priest* turn to the LORD's Table."

"Then shall the *priest*, kneeling down at the LORD's Table," etc.

"When the *priest*, standing before the holy Table . . . . he shall say the Prayer of Consecration," etc.

" Here the *priest* shall take the paten into his hands, and here to break the bread, and here to lay his hand upon all the bread."

"And here to lay his hand upon every chalice or flagon."
"The *priest* is to consecrate more bread and wine."
"The *priest* shall say the LORD's prayer."
"The *priest* (or Bishop) shall let them depart."
Priest here occurs eighteen times. The term *'minister'* occurs eight times.

III.

Declaration of the Irish Church Laity on Prayer-book Revision.

MOST certain it is, that as long as ministers are called priests, as long as they are commissioned to "forgive and retain sins," as long as they are commanded to say, "I absolve thee," however strongly the Articles, Liturgy, and Homilies witness in general against all such priestly assumptions, there will always be clergymen who will assert their right to be "priests," upon the ground of those very serious errors which our incomplete "Reformation" left in the Prayer-book. Let any man look at the priestly reaction which has set in upon the English Church during the last forty years, and say whether this statement is fanciful. For my own part, I believe that a third part of our clergy desire reunion with Rome, provided the Pope's supremacy could be curtailed. What can we hope, when learned and pious Bishops of the English Church go abroad in order to show their longings for reunion with the "*Old Catholics*," as a certain party of dissenters from Papal "infallibility" are now called? Will these Bishops, or those who follow them, propose any visible union with Presbyterian brethren, with Methodist or Baptist brethren, though these latter hold in vital union with themselves all the cardinal Gospel truths? It is too evident, from Bishop Wordsworth's letter to that *Episcopal Succession;* and the "three orders" of "Bishops, *Priests*, and Deacons," are, in his view, the one true basis of union as to Church government and order; and that all the sound Scripture doctrine taught by un-Episcopal Churches seems to go for nothing.*

In the Bishop's letter I look in vain for any repudiation of the *Priestly* system, such as "old" as well as more modern Catholics carry out. Does he then approve that ancient Priestly system? Otherwise, when he travels to hold fellowship with foreign Christians, why propose no brotherly communion with the Lutheran and Reformed Churches of Germany, France, etc.? No attempt however is made in England, or on the Continent, to embrace the "Churches of the Reformation." We must infer that our Bishops do not consider that unity in *saving truth* is sufficient, unless it is taught by an Episcopal Church. Our best English "Reformers" openly fraternised with foreign brethren in Switzerland, though the latter professed no (so-called) " Episcopal Succession," and repudiated *Priesthood.* The general doctrine as to the way of man's salvation being really ONE and the same, common sense teaches us that the way of a sinner's salvation is taught just as truly, and is just as true in itself, by the lips of a Baptist or Presbyterian, as well as by those of a Bishop, or a clergyman ordained by a Bishop.

It is consolatory to find that a large body of the laity (or brethren) in the Irish Disestablished Church, have

---

* See Bishop Wordsworth's Letter to the Secretary of the "Old Catholic" Congress. (*Times*' Newspaper of Sept. 18th, 1872.)

resolved to press for a *revised Prayer-book*, as soon as freed from the inaction in which their former state had kept them. They looked at what was dangerous to simple truth in the present Prayer-book; and since they have obtained their proper place and influence in Church Synods, we must hope that ere long their wishes will be carried out.

IV.

Upon Ordination as a needful requisite for lawful Ministry.

SINCE so much confusion and mistake prevail concerning Ordination, and since we so often hear (in this country) that some "spiritual gift" follows the imposition of hands by a "Catholic" or "Anglo-Catholic" Bishop, I will here put down all the New Testament Scriptures which bear directly upon the "laying on of hands," and the results that followed it. A right understanding of these Scriptures will remove the frequently-made objection to all *unordained* preaching, as well as other errors that are built upon the supposed virtue of Episcopal orders.

During the Apostle's ministry, there appear two kinds of "laying on of hands."

(1) The laying on of hands by *Apostles*, by which "the HOLY GHOST was given" (Acts viii. 18); *i.e.*, a spiritual gift then bestowed which the receiver had not till then possessed. Thus in Acts xix. 6, "they spake with tongues and prophesied," on whom Paul had laid his hands. Thus Acts viii. 17, when Peter and John were sent to Samaria. "They laid their hands on them (the new believers), and prayed for them, that they might

receive the HOLY GHOST. For as yet HE was fallen upon none of them." (Ver. 15—17.) To Timotheus it is written by St. Paul, "Stir up the *gift* that is in thee, by the *laying on of my hands.*" (2 Tim. i. 6.) Here was a special spiritual gift, "the SPIRIT of power and of love and of a sound mind."

Similarly we may refer to 1 Tim. iv. 14: "Neglect not the 'gift' that is in thee, which was given thee by prophecy, with the laying on of the hands of the *Presbytery.*" Here seems to be a second bestowal of spiritual powers through the laying on of hands by Apostles, *in company with the "Presbytery,"* or body of elders. These latter, as Bishop Ellicott observes, "with the Apostle, conjointly laid their hands on him." (Ellicott on 1 Tim. iv. 14, p. 65, *Notes.*) They were the Council of Elders, who met in a city like Antioch. One or more of the Apostles was present at this "laying on of hands." No mere "elder" had the power of conferring a $\chi\alpha\rho\iota\sigma\mu\alpha$, or "spiritual gift," such as is here named. From the previous verse (thirteenth) we learn that Timotheus had received the gifts of "exhortation" and of "teaching," named as gifts in Rom. xii.

(2) *The second "laying on of hands"* was that used for the ordinary commission of ministers to some spiritual office, but which conferred no new spiritual "*gift.*" Thus in Acts vi. 6, the Apostles "laid their hands" upon the seven men whom the believers had chosen to distribute alms to the widows. But previous to this their "ordination," the seven were "full of the HOLY GHOST and of wisdom." Thus Paul and Barnabas, having been called by the HOLY GHOST (Acts xiii. 3), were commended to their work with prayer, fasting, and imposition of hands. We are not told whose hands were thus imposed. It is plain, however, that on this occasion Paul needed no new spiritual "gift." From the common custom that

prevailed in the Jewish Church of laying hands upon all who were admitted to office in the synagogues, "laying on of hands" seems to have followed naturally in the appointment of Christian Church officers. The next Scripture is Acts xiv. 28. Of Paul and Barnabas it is here said, that "they *ordained* elders in every Church." Thus vaguely have our translators rendered this important verse, the only verse in the New Testament which gives any notion of the exact mode in which the ordination of elders (Bishops) was conducted. The Greek word for "ordained" is χειροτονησαντερ.

The plain first meaning of this word is, "*to appoint by a show of hands:*" i.e., by suffrages, or votes. (See Parkhurst's Greek Testament Lexicon on the Word.) Parkhurst says that it may bear a third meaning,—simply "to appoint;" but he gives us no adequate proof for this. Dean Alford, on this passage, explains the term: "The Word will not bear Jerome's or Chrysostom's sense of *laying on of hands* .... nor is there any reason for departing from the usual meaning of *electing by show of hands*. The Apostles may have elected by ordination *those Presbyters whom the Churches elected*." (Alford's Commentary, vol. ii., p. 100.) Here then seems to be the general Apostolic rule for setting apart elders or bishops (overseers). The Church elected them by vote; the Apostles, or after them, the presiding Bishop (as Timotheus) ordained them with imposition of hands. This view is strengthened by 2 Cor. viii. 19, where our translators have given the more correct meaning to χειροτονεω. "The brother who was *chosen* by the Churches:" "*appointed by vote*," would be the correct meaning. We have then here three great Scriptures for an *elective* ministry; whenever the ministers were ruling elders over Churches, "messengers" of Churches, or subordinate helpers. The deacons of Acts vi., the elders of Acts xiv., the messenger of 2 Cor. viii., were chosen for their offices according to the Church's votes.

The next great Scriptures about *ordination* are those found in 1 Tim. v. 22 and Titus i. 5. " Lay hands suddenly on no man," is the command given to Timotheus. On the exact meaning of these words learned men differ. In his valuable Commentary, Dean Alford gives a list of eminent writers, ancient and modern, who think the words to mean, "Do not *hastily* ordain men (by imposition of hands) to the ministry." (See Alford, vol. iii., p. 337.) Bishop Ellicott, on the other hand, thinks they do not refer to *ordination*, but to the too hastily receiving back of offenders into Church communion. (See Ellicott on 1 Tim. v. 22, p. 83.) Let us however suppose that *ordination* is here intended by St. Paul. If so, it proves that when an elder or deacon, having been *chosen* by the Church's votes, was brought before Timotheus for ordination, the latter was to use discretion and caution in ratifying the choice made.

Lastly, Titus is told to "*ordain* elders in every city." (Titus i. 5.) The word "ordain" is here used by our translators, no doubt, with reference to the conventional meaning which that word had acquired. The Greek word used by St. Paul is different from that used in Acts xiv. 23. It is $\kappa\alpha\theta\iota\rho\eta\mu s$: "to establish, settle, or place." This establishing of elders was doubtless crowned by prayer and solemn imposition of hands. The point, however, for our special notice is, that in these last-named cases of Timotheus and Titus, no miraculous gift, no gift of the HOLY GHOST, is said to follow the ordination of elders. Any one who reads 1 Tim. iii. and Titus i., must see that the "elder" and "deacon" had received all their qualifications from the HOLY SPIRIT *before* they could be chosen for their offices in any Church. No hint do we find given to Timotheus or Titus, that the elders on whom they laid hands would thereby "receive the HOLY GHOST;" no more than that they should receive men's *private* confessions of sin, or pronounce men's "absolution," if they judged their confessions sincere. It may have early become a doctrine, "Catholic," or generally received, that Bishops succeeded the Apostles as the channels of "spiritual gifts" to those whom they ordained. We have simply to ask, Was this doctrine *Apostolic?*—was it either enjoined in the Apostles' writings, or to be rationally deduced from them? If not, its Catholicity has no more weight than the Catholic doctrine of *Priesthood*.

If Apostolic Bishops had no such extraordinary powers, certainly no subsequent Bishops have had them. But *fact* stands up to demolish the delusive theory. We challenge all who have been ordained by Bishops in the Anglican Church, to *prove* that upon and directly following the "laying on of hands," any one "*spiritual gift*" *came upon them such as they had not before they entered the Cathedral*. Never has any honest man claimed such a miracle in his own case. On the other hand, thousands of godly men have received, and are able to use, "spiritual gifts," who have never been thus "ordained," and who know that no ordination would add to those gifts which they possess. Here are two FACTS admitting of no rational contradiction. What more is needed?

Our English Church Reformers chose the fatal course *of not going simply to the Apostles' teaching and practice* for their form of Ordination Service. They went to the so-called Catholic teaching and practice of the Roman and Greek Churches, set up long ages after the Apostles' age. They wished especially to convince the Roman Church of their own day, that they held fast to the theory of an unbroken succession of lawfully ordained Bishops, together with the unbroken continuance of the HOLY SPIRIT's grace and gifts, flowing necessarily through the "laying on of hands" by such Bishops. A child may bring this fatal theory to its logical conclusion.

If all the Roman Bishops and Priests were made valid ministers of CHRIST because their "orders" were thus DIVINELY given, what could justify the "Reformers" in removing Bishops and Priests from their lawful ministry, because the latter would not conform to the Reformed system? And again: if all Roman and Greek priests are validly appointed ministers of CHRIST during the last 1200 years of gross error in religion, then they are CHRIST's lawful ministers, though they teach *idolatrous* homage to Mary "the mother of our Lord." the fable of transubstantiation, and all other errors; while, on the other hand, all the godly ministers of non-Episcopal Churches, however bright their piety, or useful their ministry to souls, are *no lawful ministers at all!*

Thus, in our own day, Chalmers, Duff, Bonar, and Cooke, had no DIVINE sanction for their ministry. They were unlawful intruders.

V.

The Bishop of Manchester on the Ordination and Visitation Services.

Extracted from the "*Guardian*" newspaper of Dec. 11th, 1872.

N.B.—I have been kindly informed by his Lordship, that this printed report of his "charge" is authentic, being a copy of his MS.

"Some may think, and I myself am one who think, that the Form of Absolution in the Order for the

Visitation of the Sick is mediæval in its spirit rather than primitive, and seems to claim more authority for the priest than properly can belong to man; *but our* LORD's *own words to* HIS *Apostles are quite as strong.* 'Whose soever sins ye remit, they are remitted unto them; and whose soever sins ye retain, they are retained:' and no one denies that the Church has authority to declare the terms on which God has promised to forgive sins, and to give, in the same sense in which Nathan gave it to David, to the penitent sinner 'the benefit of absolution.' 'The Lord hath put away thy sin; thou shalt not die.' Even the phrase in the form of the Ordering of Priests, which has been so much cavilled at, 'Receive the Holy Ghost for the office and work of a priest in the Church of God, now committed unto thee by the imposition of our hands,' is no mere arrogant and indefensible claim of the Bishop and the assisting Presbyters to possess, or to have the power to bestow, supernatural powers,—is nothing more than Paul claims, when he bids Timothy, the young Ephesian Bishop, 'stir up the gift of God, which was in him, by the putting on of his hands, together with the laying on of the hands of the Presbytery.' 'If,' as Richard Hooker says, 'the Holy Ghost, which our Saviour in His first ordinations gave, doth still concur with spiritual vocations throughout all ages,' 'seeing that the same power is now given, why should the same form of words expressing it be thought *foolish?* Remove what these *foolish words* do imply, and what hath the ministry of God besides wherein to glory?'"

Unless the Bishop had vouched for the accuracy of this printed report, I could not have believed that so enlightened a writer could have used these words. "Because our DIVINE LORD was pleased to invest HIS Apostles with powers supernatural, *therefore* an ordinary clergyman, or "priest," may say to a dying man, "*I absolve thee from all thy sins.*" There seems to be an equal want of reverence and of reasoning in the statement. The grand point is simply here taken for granted: viz., That any men *or all ordained ministers had such power granted to them after the Apostles.* No proof is ventured for this unconditional statement.

Next, if we take the Apostles as being endowed with extraordinary powers, we never read of their saying to the people who professed their faith in the LORD JESUS, "I, Paul, or Peter, absolve you." It is, "Through this man is preached unto you the forgiveness of sins." (Acts xiii. 38.) " If we confess our sins, HE is faithful and just to forgive us our sins." (1 John i. 9.) Into the full import of these DIVINE words, " Whose sins ye remit," etc., as then spoken, I cannot here enter. It would require a long discussion. Whatever our view of them, "supernatural power" was given thereby, though not to the full extent of the Pentecostal effusion of the SPIRIT.

(1) The Bishop considers this Form of Absolution "rather *mediæval than primitive.*" By "*primitive*" we generally understand the third and fourth centuries, when Apostolic traditions might be kept in a measure uncorrupted. I say "might be;" for we have already seen how Clement and Ignatius fell from Apostolic simplicity. *Mediæval* tradition is certainly to be suspected: *mediæval* religion included all Rome's errors. We find, in fact, that the priestly formula, "I absolve thee," was *not* used, even in the corrupted Western Church, before the twelfth century; and the author who first wrote in its defence was Thomas Aquinas, the celebrated champion (as we may call him) of Rome's accumulated errors. So that this dangerous formula of " absolution " is really a creation of modern Rome; and yet Cranmer adopted it. (See in proof Palmer's "*Origines Liturgica,*" vol. ii.

Humphry's "Historical Treatise on the Prayer-book, p. 252, third edition.) WHEATLEY (on the Prayer-book) says (p. 435, on the Visitation Service), "It does not appear to have been generally introduced till about the middle of the *twelfth* century; and then it was made use of to reconcile the penitent to the Church. Within a century afterwards, indeed, it was a ruled case in the Church, that such as received the confession of penitents should, by an *indicative* form, absolve them from all their sins:" *i.e.*, as the Roman priest does absolve *judicially*. To this modern Roman formula was our unhappy National Church committed by those Reformers who temporised with error.

(2) "No one denies that *the Church* has authority to declare the terms on which GOD has promised to forgive sins; and to give in the same sense in which Nathan gave it to David,—'The LORD hath put away thy sin. Thou shalt not die.'" I can see no parallel between Nathan's commission and that of ordinary pastors and Bishops. Nathan was an *inspired* prophet, sent to deliver to men messages of the DIVINE will, communicated supernaturally to himself. Bishops are *not* thus inspired: they have no supernatural messages to deliver. *Secondly,* though a man inspired, Nathan did not say, as clergymen are told to say, "I absolve thee from all thy sins;" but "the LORD hath put away thy sin." We have no objection to ministers "declaring to HIS people, *being penitent*, the absolution of their sins." They do so, however, not as judges, or inquisitors of the heart by process of a confessional, as do the Romish priests.

(3) "Even the phrase in the Form of Ordering of Priests, which has been so much cavilled at, 'Receive the HOLY GHOST for the office and work of a *priest* .... by the imposition of our hands,' is *no mere arrogant and indefensible claim* of the Bishop, and of the assisting

Presbyters, *to possess, or to have the power to bestow, supernatural powers,* is nothing more than Paul claims, when he bids Timothy, the watchful Bishop, to 'stir up the gift of GOD that was in him, by the putting on of his hands, together with the laying on of the hands of the Presbytery.'" (Hooker is then quoted by the Bishop as confirming his statement.)

Here, as in the former case, the point in dispute is taken for granted, without any proof. The statement is mere assertion. The *question* remains. Does the power of conferring "gifts" of the SPIRIT necessarily attend a Bishop in ordination, because a "gift" was given to Timothy through St. Paul's hands? "Through the laying on of Apostles' hands, the HOLY GHOST was given." (Acts viii.) Such is the DIVINE record. But we read of *no other men* to whom such power was "handed down," or was to be given. We deny the *fact* of such *miraculous power being given to any but Apostles.* We challenge proof of the gift: and we cannot allow those who claim its possession to persevere in such claim without remonstrance.

In answer to a letter which I wrote to the Bishop, and to which he courteously replied, he says that he purposely "*excluded* the arrogant and indefensible claim of the Bishop to bestow supernatural powers," etc.; that "whatever power was transmitted in ordination, was the same that Paul told Timothy to stir up." As I informed the Bishop in my reply, ordinary Bishops and the Apostle are thus put by him upon a level. What Paul gave, a Bishop gives. Such a statement only begs the main question at issue. Timothy, by St. Paul's hands, had really received "the SPIRIT of love and of power and of a sound mind." (2 Tim. i. 6.) Clergymen do not receive such a gift (as far as evidence goes) at or through a Bishop's ordination. I could not but remind the Bishop to what a grave conclusion these views of "ordination" must lead us. If spiritual grace and gifts must follow on the imposition of hands by a Bishop, then all the priests of Rome and the Greek Church, who for centuries have taught an idolatrous worship of Mary, have received such spiritual grace and gifts. On the other hand, such men as Challoners, Duff, and McCheyne, because they were ordained by ministers who had themselves had no Episcopal ordination, received neither grace nor gifts, and had no authority to minister. This theory excommunicates all good ministers of most foreign Reformation Churches.

VI.

On "Lay Readers."

SEVERAL English Bishops lately sent forth what are called "Lay Readers." Their office is (as I understand) to explain as well as to read the Scriptures, to visit the sick and the poor, in those parishes where the clergyman approves of such ministry. Though so long delayed, such a *deaconship* (as we may call it) is an excellent improvement. But for this office there is no canon, formulary, or *legal* sanction; and as long as Bishops are bound by the strict obligations of an *Establishment*, they cannot legally impose new officers upon clergymen, or upon their parishioners. The Lay Readers are also forbidden to *preach*. We must, however, rejoice that the *principle* of a long forbidden lay agency is at last admitted.

LONDON : WILLIAM HUNT AND COMPANY.

MARCH, 1873.

SELECTION FROM

The New Publications of

WILLIAM HUNT AND COMPANY.

Biblical, Practical, and Expository.

Thoughts on the Christian Life;
or, Leaves from Letters. By the late Hetty Bowman, Author of "Christian Daily Life," etc. With Introduction by Mrs. Gordon, Author of "The Home Life of Sir David Brewster," etc. Second Edition. Crown 8vo. 3s. 6d.

The Nature and Evidences of Regeneration.
By the Rev. George Townshend Fox, M.A. With a Preface by the Rev. Octavius Winslow, D.D., Incumbent of Emmanuel Church, Brighton. Limp cloth, red edges, 1s. 9d.; extra cloth, bevelled boards, gilt edges, 2s. 6d.

Life in the Ghetto;
or, the Jewish Physician. By the Author of "Doing and Suffering," and "Broad Shadows in Life's Pathway," and uniform in size. 5s.

The Track of the Light;
or, Christ's Footsteps Followed. By the Rev. J. George Bullock, M.A., Rector of St. Runwald's, Colchester. 2s.

Veins of Silver;
or, Treasures Hid beneath the Surface. By Samuel Garratt, M.A., Vicar of St. Margaret's, Ipswich; Author of "A Commentary on the Revelation of St. John," "Signs of the Times," etc. Post 8vo. 4s. 6d.

Christian Chivalry;
or, the Armour of God on the Soldier of the Cross. By the Rev. Samuel Garratt, M.A. Small 8vo. Extra cloth, 3s.

Carrying Things to Extremes.
By the Author of "Copsley Annals." Square 16mo, cloth, red edges. 1s.

WILLIAM HUNT AND COMPANY,

Signs of the Times;
Showing that the Coming of the Lord Draweth Near. Second edition. By Samuel Garratt, M.A., Vicar of St. Margaret's, Ipswich; Author of "A Commentary on the Revelation of St. John," etc. F'cap 8vo., extra cloth, 2s. 6d.

The Religion of Redemption;
or, the Doctrine of Man's Ruin and Christ's Salvation, Defined and Defended. A Contribution to the Preliminaries of Christian Apology. By R. W. Monsell, B.A., late Pastor of the Free Church of Neufchatel, Switzerland. Second Edition. With Life of the Author by the Rev. J. B. Heard, M.A. 1 vol. 8vo., 10s.

"Dies Iræ!"
The Judgment of the Great Day, viewed in the light of Scripture and Conscience. By R. B. Girdlestone, M.A., Author of "The Anatomy of Scepticism." Crown 8vo. 6s.

Reminiscences of a Clergyman during a Ministry
of Forty Years in a Country Parish. By the Rev. Robert Grant, B.C.L., Prebendary of Salisbury Cathedral, Fellow of Winchester College, and Vicar of Bradford Abbes.

Our Father.
A Word of Encouraging Remembrance for the Children of God. By the Author of "Thoughts on Conversion." With an Introduction by the Rev. A. Hewlett, D.D., Vicar of Astley, near Manchester. Second edition. Cloth extra, bevelled boards. 3s.

Islington Conference Papers, 1872.
Revised by the several Authors. With Introduction by the Rev. Daniel Wilson, M.A., Vicar. Published at the Request of the Meeting. Crown 8vo. Cloth boards, 2s. 6d.

The Intermediate State of the Blessed Dead;
in a Series of Meditational Expositions. By the Rev. Joseph Baylee, D.D. Second edition, enlarged. Cloth extra, 3s. 6d.

The Ministry of Home;
or, Brief Expository Lectures on Divine Truth. Designed especially for Family and Private Reading. By Octavius Winslow, D.D. Crown 8vo. 5s. Extra binding, gilt edges, 6s.

Christian Experience;
 or, Words of Loving Counsel and Sympathy. Selected from the Remains of the late Mrs. Mary Winslow. Edited by her Son, Rev. Octavius Winslow, D.D. Small 8vo. 3s.

The Faithful Witness?
 Being Expository Lectures on the Epistles to the Seven Churches of Asia. By R. W. Forrest, M.A., St. Jude's, Kensington. Crown 8vo., 6s.

Elisha the Prophet a Type of Christ.
 By the Rev. Dr. Edersheim. Crown 8vo. 3s. 6d.

The Finding of the Saviour in the Temple.
 An Exposition of Luke ii. 46—51. Based upon, and explanatory of, Holman Hunt's great Sacred Picture. By the Rev. Richard Glover, M.A., Vicar of St. Luke's, West Holloway. Crown 8vo., 4s.; gilt edges, 4s. 6d.

Sunshine and Shadow.
 Poems by Jennette Threlfall. With Introduction by the Lord Bishop of Lincoln. Small Post 8vo. 5s.

Wayside Wisdom for Wayfarers;
 or, Voices from Silent Teachers. By the Author of "Hymns for the Household of Faith." With Introduction by Mrs. Sewell. 3s. 6d.

For Mothers' Meetings and Bible Classes.

A Message.
 An Arrow from a Bow drawn at a venture. Large Type. Post 8vo. Limp cloth, 1s.; paper cover, 8d.

Hearts made glad and Homes made happy.
 Sketches of Subjects for Mothers' Meetings and Fathers' Classes. Post 8vo. Extra cloth. 3s. 6d.

Seed Scattered Broadcast;
 or, Incidents in a Camp Hospital. By S. McBeth. With an Introduction, and Edited by the Author of "The Memorials of Capt. Hedley Vicars." Uniform with "English Hearts and English Hands." Second edition. Post 8vo., 3s. 6d. Cheap issue, limp cloth. 2s.

Simple Readings on the Gospels.
  Arranged in Daily Portions for the use of Families and Schools. Compiled from the Works of the Rev. Canon Ryle, Rev. Albert Barnes, and other Expository writers. By A. S. F. One vol., extra cloth, 7s. ; or vol. I., 3s. 6d. ; II., 4s.

Suggestive Readings on the Gospel of St. John.
  With Copious Notes and References. By Mrs. Hamilton, Author of "Suggestive Readings on St. Luke." 2s. 6d.

Suggestive Readings with my Sunday-school Teachers,
  on the Gospel of St. Luke. With Copious Notes and References. Post 8vo. 2s.

The Christian Life.
  Viewed under some of its more Practical Aspects. By the Rev. Sir Emilius Bayley, Bart., Vicar of St. John's, Paddington. F'cap 8vo. Extra cloth, 3s. ; gilt edges, 3s. 6d.

The Home of Poverty made Rich.
  A volume of Interest specially adapted for Mothers' Meetings. By Mrs. Best, Author of "Tracts on the Parables," etc. Second edition. F'cap 8vo. With Frontispiece. 2s. 6d. Cheap issue, limp cloth, 1s. 6d.

The Rock,
  and other Short Lectures on Passages of Holy Scripture. By Miss Hasell, Dalemain ; Author of "Saturday Afternoons." Dedicated to Sir George Musgrave, Bart. F'cap 8vo. 2s.

Seasons of Sickness and Sorrow.
BY THE LATE MISS CHARLOTTE ELLIOTT,
Author of "Just as I am."

Hours of Sorrow Cheered and Comforted.
  Poems for the Season of Affliction. Seventh edition. F'cap 8vo. Toned paper. Extra binding, 3s.

Morning and Evening Hymns for a Week.
  Fortieth thousand. Limp cloth, gilt edges. 1s.

Thoughts in Verse, on Sacred Subjects.
  With some Miscellaneous Poems. Written in early years, and now first published. Small 8vo. Extra binding. 4s.

Hymn-book for the Sick.
  In large type, with texts of Scripture. By the Rev. W. O. Purton, B.A., Rector of Kingston-on-Sea. Limp cloth, 1s. Paper, 6d.

Short Sermons for Sick Rooms.
In very large Type. By the Rev. Josiah Bateman, M.A., Vicar of Margate, Hon. Canon of Canterbury, and Rural Dean, Author of the "Life of Henry Venn Elliott, of Brighton," etc. Crown 8vo. Limp cloth, extra, 2s. Extra cloth, gilt edges, 2s. 6d.

Songs in Suffering:
or, the Voice of Trust and Praise in Sickness and Sorrow. By the Rev. W. O. Purton, B.A., Rector of Kingston-on-Sea. F'cap 8vo., cloth boards, 3s.; cloth extra, bevelled boards, gilt edges, 3s. 6d.

Sun-Glints in the Wilderness.
Our Lord's Temptation, and other subjects. By the Rev. Hugh Macmillan, LL.D., Author of "Bible Teachings in Nature." Crown 8vo. 4s. 6d.

Trust in Trial:
or, Lessons of Peace in the School of Affliction. Meditations, with Prayers and Hymns for the Sick and Suffering. By the Rev. W. O. Purton, B.A., Rector of Kingston-on-Sea. Third edition. Large type. Fcap. 8vo. Cloth, 1s. 6d.; extra cloth, 2s.

BY THE REV. GEORGE EVERARD, M.A.,
Vicar of St. Mark's, Wolverhampton.

Day by Day;
or, Counsels to Christians on the Details of Every Day Life. With Introduction by the Rev. T. Vores, Incumbent of St. Mary's Hastings. Sixth edition. F'cap 8vo. Cloth, red edges, 3s.; antique, gilt edges, 3s. 6d. Cheap edition. Uniform with "Not Your Own." 1s. 6d.

Home Sundays;
or, Help and Consolation from the Sanctuary. Cloth extra, 3s.; bevelled, gilt edges, 3s. 6d.

"Not Your Own;"
or, Counsels to Young Christians. Sixth edition. 18mo., cloth limp, 1s.; extra binding, 1s. 6d.

Safe and Happy.
Words of Help and Encouragement to Young Women, with Prayers for Daily use. Second edition. Uniform with "Not Your Own," etc. Limp cloth, 1s.; extra cloth, gilt edges, 1s. 6d.

The Home of Bethany;
or, Christ Revealed as the Teacher and Comforter of His People. Uniform with "Not Your Own." Limp cloth, 1s.; extra cloth, gilt edges, 1s. 6d.

Welcome Home!
or, Plain Teachings from the Story of the Prodigal. Large 32mo., cloth limp, 6d.; extra binding, red edges, 8d.

WILLIAM HUNT AND COMPANY,

BY THE REV. J. C. RYLE, M.A.,
Honorary Canon of Norwich;
Vicar of Stradbroke, and Rural Dean of Hoxne, Suffolk.

Expository Thoughts on the Gospels.
Designed for Family and Private Reading, with the Text complete, and copious Notes.

ST. MATTHEW. Extra cloth. 6s.	ST. LUKE. Vol. II. 7s.
ST. MARK. Uniform with the above 5s.	ST. JOHN. Vol. I. 6s. 6d.
	ST. JOHN. Vol. II. 6s. 6d.
ST. LUKE. Vol. I. 5s. 6d.	ST. JOHN. Vol. III. 8s.

This work is also kept in half Morocco, at an excess of 3s. per volume. In extra half Morocco binding, at 5s. 6d.; or whole Turkey Morocco, 6s. 6d. per volume. Also in extra bindings, for presentation.

Bishops and Clergy of Other Days.
With an Introduction on the Real Merits of the Reformers and Puritans. Crown 8vo., extra cloth, 4s.

Lessons from English Church History.
A Lecture delivered in the Town Hall, Oxford, on Monday, May 1st, 1871. The Provost of Oriel in the Chair. With Appendix, giving the opinions of some well-known English Divines on the Controversy about the Lord's Supper. 56pp. Crown 8vo. Paper cover, 6d. Limp cloth, 1s.

Coming Events and Present Duties.
Being Miscellaneous Sermons and Addresses on Prophetical Subjects; arranged, revised, and corrected. Crown 8vo. 3s. 6d.

Home Truths.
Being the Miscellaneous Addresses and Tracts, revised and corrected especially for this work. Sixth Edition. F'cap 8vo., extra cloth, lettered. Eight Series. Each illustrated with a Frontispiece and Vignette Title. Each volume, 3s. 6d.

This work is also kept in Morocco, Russia, and other elegant bindings, for presents; prices and specimens of which will be forwarded on application to the Publishers.

Hymns for the Church on Earth.
Being Three Hundred Hymns, for the most part of modern date. Selected and arranged by the Rev. J. C. Ryle, M.A. Ninth Edition.

In small 8vo., black cloth, red edges, 4s.; limp cloth, for invalids, 4s.; black antique, 4s. 6d.; violet and extra cloth antique, gilt edges, 5s.; Turkey Morocco, 10s. 6d. Also in Russia and other bindings, for presentation.

A Portable Edition of "Hymns for the Church on Earth."
Printed on toned paper. Extra cloth, gilt edges, 3s. 6d.; red edges, 3s.

Story of Madame Thérèse, the Cantinière;
or, the French Army in '92. Translated from the work of M. M. Erckmann-Chatrain, by two Sisters. With an Introduction and Edited by the Rev. J. C. Ryle, M.A. With nineteen full-page Engravings. Crown 8vo. 3s. 6d.

A detailed List of all Tracts by the Rev. J. C. Ryle may be obtained on application to the Publishers.

HOLLES STREET, CAVENDISH SQUARE.

BY BROWNLOW NORTH, B.A.,
Magdalen Hall, Oxford; Registrar of the Diocese of Winchester and Surrey.

Think on These Things;
　Wisdom: her cry—Wisdom: who has it ?—The Grace of God—Christ the Saviour: Christ the Judge. Uniform with "Ourselves." 3s.

The Prodigal Son;
　or, the Way Home. Cloth boards, extra, antique binding. 2s.

Ourselves:
　A Picture sketched from the History of the Children of Israel. Fourth edition. Cloth boards, 2s. 6d.; antique bindings, 3s. Fifth and cheaper edition, 18mo., cloth limp, 1s. 9d.

Yes! or No!
　or, God's Offer of Salvation. (Gen. xxiv. 58.) Uniform with "Ourselves." Third edition. Extra cloth, 3s. Cloth limp, cheap edition, 1s. 9d.

The Rich Man and Lazarus.
　A Practical Exposition. Uniform with "Ourselves." Second edition. Square 18mo, cloth boards, 1s. 6d.; antique, 2s.

You! what You are, and what You may be.
　Sketched from the History of the Gadarene. Extra cloth, 1s.

Uniform Series of Large Type Books. Each Sixpence.

God's Way of Salvation.
Earnest Words: New and Old. A Series of Addresses. With Prayers and Hints for Christians.
Gathered Leaves.
Think! Earnest Words for the Thoughtless.
The Grace of God. Thoughts on Titus ii. 11—19.
Wisdom: her cry. A Commentary on Proverbs i. 21—33.
Wisdom: who has it? An Exposition on 1 Corinthians i.
Words for the Anxious. Second Edition.
The Good Physician, and other Short Papers on Important Subjects.
Christ the Saviour,—Christ the Judge. John v. 16—30.
Leaves. A series of Tracts in very Large Type, for General Distribution. In packets of 50 assorted. 6d.
More Leaves. A Packet of Four-page Tracts for General Distribution.

BY THE REV. GORDON CALTHROP, M.A.,
Vicar of St. Augustine's, Highbury New Park, London.

The Lost Sheep Found,
　and other Sermons. Preached to the Children of St. Augustine's Church, London. By the Rev. Gordon Calthrop, M.A. Second edition. 18mo. 3s.

Pulpit Recollections.
　Being Sermons preached during a Six Years' Ministry at Cheltenham and Highbury New Park. Revised and adapted for general reading. One vol. Post 8vo. 5s. 6d.

Lectures on Home Subjects.
　Addressed especially to the Working Classes. F'cap 8vo. 2s. 6d.

Words Spoken to my Friends.
　Twenty-four Sermons.　　　　　　　　　　　　　　　[In the press.

EVENING HOURS.

Edited by the Rev. E. H. BICKERSTETH, M.A.

MONTHLY. Large 8vo. 64pp. PRICE SIXPENCE. Well Illustrated.

ARRANGEMENTS FOR 1873.

Bet of Stowe: a Serial Tale of the last century, founded on fact. By Lady Barker.

Round the Tower. Dark Shadows of London Life; or, Human Existence East of the City. By J. Weylland, Author of "The Man with the Book," etc.

Glimpses of America. By John S. Howson, D.D., Dean of Chester.

Chief Women. By Mrs. Gordon, Author of "The Home Life of Sir David Brewster."

Germs of Thought from my Note-book. By Hugh Macmillan, LL.D., F.R.S E.

Incidents of Hospital Life. By the Author of "The Life of the Rev. Dr. Marsh."

Serial Story of the Wisconsin Fires. By the Author of 'Broad Shadows on Life's Pathway.' [In Preparation.]

A Visit to Moab. By the Rev. Canon Tristram, LL.D., F.R.S.

The Bridal of the Spirits: a Romaunt. By the Rev. P. B. Power.

Leaders of the Quietist movement in France. By A. M. James, Author of "Christian Counsels." [Ryle.

Biographical Sketches of Divines. By the Rev. Canon

In the Track of Christian Charity. By Rev. Gordon Calthrop.

A New Serial Tale for the Young. By the Author of the "Wide Wide World." [Will also be commenced early in the year.]

Heroines of the Poets. By L. Madeline, Esq.

The Romance of Missions. By the Rev. H. Stern, and others.

Kit Mowbray; or, This Generation. By A. C. Ewald, F.S.A., Author of "Life and Times of Algernon Sydney," etc.

Jottings from the Fathers. By Professor Mayor, late Librarian of Cambridge.

Parables for Children, and other Papers. By the Editor.

Addresses to Public School Boys. By Public Men.

Hymnody, Church Music, and Poetry. By Dr. Gauntlett, J. T. Cooper, Esq., Rev. R. Wilton, Miss Havergal, J. Threlfall, etc.

In addition to the above, articles will be contributed by—

The Lord Bishop of Ripon.
R. Dudley Baxter, Esq.
The Rev. Canon Bell, M.A.
The Rev. Dr. Edersheim.

J. Macgregor, Esq. (Rob Roy.)
The Rev. A. W. Thorold, M.A.
The Author of "Copsley Annals."
Miss E. J. Whately, etc., etc.

London: William Hunt and Company, 23, Holles Street, W.

www.ingramcontent.com/pod-product-compliance
Lightning Source LLC
Chambersburg PA
CBHW031444160426
43195CB00010BB/836